Nights by the Wall

Nights by the Wall

A Guide to Dreams, Dreamwork, and
Profound Self-Knowing

Barbara Black Koltuv, Ph.D

NICOLAS-HAYS, INC
Lake Worth, FL

Published in 2011 by
NICOLAS-HAYS, INC.
P. O. Box 540206 • Lake Worth, FL 33454-0206
www.nicolashays.com
Distributed to the trade by Red Wheel/Weiser, LLC
65 Parker St., Unit 7 • Newburyport, MA 01950-4600
www.redwheelweiser.com

All dreams and journal entries are used with the express permission of the dreamers and dream journalists who wish to remain anonymous. None of the dreamers are analysands of the author.

Library of Congress Cataloging-in-Publication Data available upon request

978-089254-151-5

Cover and text design by Kathryn Sky-Peck

Cover art © Baruch Nachshon of Hebron, from a series entitled "Redemption."
Used by kind permission of the artist. www.nachshonart.com.

Printed in the United States of America
VG

7 6 5 4 3 2 1

Contents

For all who are dear to me—
You know who you are!

Introduction

I was the kind of kid who wished on stars and four leaf clovers, and was fascinated by puzzles, mysteries, and stories. I think I was born that way. Astrologers have told me that my birth chart shows I've had to choose between being fully my Self, or being the child my mother wished me to be. I chose the inner, mystic way, "Chose" is much too rational a word for this. I believe that I am who I was meant to be.

I grew up in Crown Heights in Brooklyn. During the Second World War there was a tiny group of Lubuvitcher Chassidim living nearby on Eastern Parkway. After the war, when I was six or seven, the Catholic Archdiocese of New York arranged with the New York City Board of Education to offer Religious Instruction to Public School children. The Lubuvitchers followed their lead, and with the parents' permission, they began to gather up children from the Public Schools on Wednesday afternoons at 2 o'clock, and take them to a small shul for a couple of hours of religious instruction. I begged my parents to let me go.

So it happened that a small group of us were collected from our Public School by the Lubuvitchers and taken down the street to David ben Gershon, a mysterious, magical place. It was a strange, dim, narrow room, smelling of old books and men. There was an eternal flame burning in a brass lamp. There were blue velvet curtains covering the Ark where the Torah was stored. On those curtains, embroidered in faded gold thread, were the two tablets Moses brought down from Mount Sinai, the Ten Commandments written in Hebrew letters. The words were enclosed on either side by magnificent golden lions. The curtain covering the Ark of the Covenant was only the beginning of the beauty. Behind the curtain, in its own blue velvet, gold embroidered case, was the magnificent parchment Torah, a scroll with wooden staves, with beautiful fiery letters in shiny black ink with little crowns on them.

We sat right down in front of the Ark and the old Rebbe —with a beard and a hat, and enormous loving-kindness—told us the Torah stories with the sweetness of honey. In this small, dark sanctuary these stories were real to me. I could see Gan Eden, Adam and Eve and the serpent, Cain killing his brother, the wilderness of Bamidbar, the tents in the desert, and Jacob's dream of the angels climbing up and down the ladder.

During the same period of my childhood I also attended the story hour at the Children's Library at Grand Army Plaza. This was a beautiful, modern building, with lovely bronze gates with sculpted squirrels. The Brooklyn Public Library was set on the edge of the Botanical Gardens, and furnished in art deco blond wood. The story telling took place in a glass-walled balcony room overlooking the main reading room. The stories I heard there were classic fairy tales. I loved hearing them, but they were not real to me. The Torah stories were.

There was not much religious practice in my house. What I do recall was my sense of awe each year when I came upon the soft flame of the Yahrtzeit candle burning on the anniversary of the death of my father's father. He had died when my dad was five, and his little brother was three. The fear that my father would die colored my childhood and lasted long into my adult years. For me the Yahrtzeit candle was associated with night terrors. It must have been lit at sundown after I was asleep. There it would be, in a special glass on the refrigerator, burning all night long in the otherwise dark apartment.

At some point in analysis—I think when I was about twenty—I began to understand what all this was about. Although my mother loved me and did the best she could for me, my mother wanted a very different sort of child. I was too intense for her nature. My father loved me just as I was. At a very early age I had to sacrifice my mother's love, in order to be myself. That is why I was so preoccupied as a child with wishing, and praying, and God. And that is why I was so taken by the stories we were told by the Lubuvitcher rebbe. The Lubuvitcher rebbe made me feel loved by God. I think I knew that God loved me as my father did, but that God was much older, and much more almighty than my father. I always prayed to God to keep my father safe.

We celebrated Chanukah with latkes and candle lighting at home, and Passover with my entire family at my grandparents' houses with great warmth, and delicious special meals. Somehow, even though there were readings from the Hagadah, and I knew the stories, I never quite associated those feasts and family get-togethers with God. I knew we were Jewish, but no one ever mentioned God. I, on the other hand kept up a steady dialogue of prayer, wishing and just plain wondering about God.

The neighborhood I grew up in was half Jewish and half Catholic. I had no understanding of the differences and similarities between our faiths. It was all just images out of context. The Catholic families were large—sometimes with as many as six children—the Jewish families smaller, usually with only two children. The Catholics would hang a purple and black wreath on the door when someone died. There was a church and a parochial school on the next block. There was a crucifix outside the church with a bleeding Jesus on the cross. I was very afraid of that and contrived not to walk past it. I had no idea that Catholics or Jesus had anything to do with God. There were often nuns in my neighborhood covered from head to toe in black habits with something white framing their faces. They were always in twos, and I was always afraid of them. I once overheard two of them talking in the hardware store. I was on the other side of a tall island of shelving and heard one say to the other, "She lost her mother." I knew it meant something terrible. I thought it was even worse than death.

When I was about eight years old, I read a book about a girl named Maida who got the measles. Her parents were afraid that she would go blind and kept her in a darkened room. Then she was visited by angels who took her away, and she died. It never occurred to me that this had anything to do with God. When I got the measles, I was afraid of going blind, and not being able to read. I did not worry about dying.

There were trolley cars on the avenue at the end of my block. They ran on tracks, with an inverted V-shaped thing on top that connected to an overhead cable, and sometimes they sparked. I thought the whole thing was magical and I tried to keep an image of trolley cars running along continuously in my mind. I thought of them as being a sort of background for whatever else I was thinking, and I would frequently check to make sure they were there and moving. I never wanted to lose sight of them or forget about them. It was very important to me to be able to do the two things at once—to keep the trolley cars moving and to think about something else as well. Later I realized that the trolleys ran on electricity, and the connection of above and below was what kept them moving horizontally. As a kid though, I did not think that trolley cars had anything to do with God, or what one of my Jungian analysts later called electricity—"a transpersonal source." For me as a child, God was personal, a resource, and a refuge.

When I was twelve I read a book of my mother's called *Love and Psychoanalysis.* It was all about dreams and sex. I knew then that I would be a psychoanalyst and study dreams and stories for the rest of my life.

I studied psychology as an undergraduate, and then as a doctoral candidate in the clinical psychology program at Columbia, and later in the New York University Post Doctoral Program in Psychoanalysis with classical Freudian analysts, Neo-Freudians, Sullivanians, Existentialist analysts and others.

I learned about the personal, and the interpersonal, but by the late 1960s I was beginning to need the *transpersonal* as well. I had never been a Freudian, or a Sullivanian, nor did I adopt any of the other theoretical positions that were popular at that time. My teachers said, "You are very talented, but you do analysis by the seat of your pants." That was so. I was deeply committed to dreamwork, journal writing, drawing, painting, stories, novels and folklore, but I did not have a theoretical position. The consciousness-raising groups of the Women's Movement, the sixties mantra "Make love, not war!", the incredible explosion of the political as personal—these all touched a deep chord in me. I found my own voice. I began to think and write from the heart. For me the spiritual was personal. Meaning supplanted understanding. Then I found C. G. Jung, and a theory that made sense, or at least encompassed sense, for me.

After years of doing dreams—by the seat of my pants, with a doctorate in clinical psychology, and a diploma in psychoanalysis from respected universities, sitting behind our hippy-dippy cabin on our sixty acres of Catskill big woods, reading the Whole Earth Catalogue—I came upon Jung writing about the value of one's own memories, dreams, and reflections:

> Often, when I was alone, I sat down on this stone , and then began an imaginary game that went something like this: "I am sitting on top of this stone and it is underneath." But the stone could also say "I" and think: "I am lying here on this slope and he is sitting on top of me." The question then arose: "Am I the one who is sitting on the stone, or am I the stone on which he is sitting?" (C. G. Jung, *Memories, Dreams, Reflections*, 20-21)

And a few paragraphs later, Jung wrote about a secret amulet that he had made and hidden in a forbidden place. This man, I knew, understood the very essence of psychoanalysis.

Immediately, the "seat of my pants" became a soulful inner knowing that has informed my life and work to this day.

"That you live for God," writes Jung in a letter to Walter Robert Corti "is perhaps the healthiest thing about you . . ."

When I was in the clinical psychology program at Columbia, the emphasis was on scientist, not practitioner. As a top student I had a United States Public Health Service grant. It entitled me to full tuition and a small stipend. I used my grant to pay for as many clinical courses I could take at NYU's clinical psychology program. There the faculty included many trained analysts, and the teaching emphasis was on "practitioner" and "clinician." By the time I had my doctorate from Columbia, NYU had begun the first university-based program in psychoanalysis and I was a member of the first full class. However, even there I was considered a bit wild and atheoretical. It was at NYU that they told me, "You are a gifted analyst, but you do dreams by the seat of your pants." At Columbia, Jung was considered in one third of a chapter in a text on *Theories of Personality*, and was dismissed as a mystic and an anti-Semite. At NYU, Jung was mentioned only as an anti-Semite and a mystic. Jung or not, by then I knew that for me dreams were as Freud had said, "the royal road to the unconscious," and as my brilliant supervisor, analyst Erich Fromm, taught, "The Forgotten Language." Dreams became the deep rich source of my own analysis, and my work with patients.

Many years later I dreamed:

I am at 1030 Carroll Street, the large apartment house where my parents lived when I was born. Inside I find a gorgeous old synagogue. The walls are lacquered deep red and festooned with antique gold. I did not know it was here. "God was in this place and I did not know it," Jacob said after dreaming of the angels ascending and descending the ladder between above and below. Modern Orthodox young women are beginning to fill the beautiful synagogue. It is the dwelling place of the Shekhina, the womb of my true mother.

The words. . . . "I found him whom my heart loves. I held him fast, nor would I let him go till I had brought him into my mother's house, into the room of her who conceived me," says the female lover in Song of Songs. . .

I go out on to Carroll Street where I lived as baby. It is dark. I feel my way. I know the way. There is moonlight. Laila/Lilah is my name in Arabic and Hebrew. Both mean night. I am at home in the night and in the world of dreams.

I turn a corner and come to the top of a hill. It is noon. There is a very well marked archeological park with museums and clearly documented excavated areas at several levels. I walk down a little, then sit and begin to slide down by the seat of my pants. This is how I always understood dreams. I realize that there will come a place where there is a depression in the hillside and then I will fly. I can do it! It is all right. I will land on my seat which is padded enough for this short flight.

I follow my dreams. In the place of my beginnings, perhaps even because of my mother's narcissism, there was a dwelling place for the Shekhina, and even now, that way is open to me. The modern orthodox young women use it and I can follow in their footsteps. I find the hillside across from my childhood home already excavated and well marked. At noon in my life, after years of dreamwork, this part of my story is known to me.

PART ONE

Foundation

Nights by the Wall

The last remaining wall of the ancient temple in Jerusalem is the Western Wall, also called the Wailing Wall or the *kotel*. For me it is the place of dreams and soulful dreamwork. At the Wall, we offer up our prayers to God, and at the Wall, if we listen closely, we can hear the voice of God within us. When I work with patients to unravel the meaning in dreams, I am merely acting as a conduit, a listening heart—a Wailing Wall—between the patient and the hidden voice waiting to be heard within the soul. Through our dreams we can connect to the divine spark within ourselves; we can come to know our whole Self in a complete and truthful way. Simply writing down our dreams, and allowing them to matter, opens a sacred pathway to healing and wholeness.

Dreams are a gift from God and treated as such, soulful dreamwork brings integration, healing, and joy. Dreams are the heart's knowledge and the guiding words of the soul. They give us a symbol system and a personal soul language by which we can know and become our most authentic self.

This book is both a meditation and a guidebook. After years of working with analysands and helping the dreamer understand the dream, I have come to see myself as the Wall—the conduit—comforting and solid, yet essentially unnecessary to another soul on his or her path to self awareness. We all have to ability to listen to and be guided by our dreams.

This book is both a memoir of my own journey into dreamwork as well a map for those who wish to travel the path; to delve into dreamwork to pursue their own path to self knowing. Because dreams are a sacred gift, a sacred language, to bring you along on my journey I have drawn upon the tradition that has informed my life: Judaism. I have purposefully let the book be written in a dreamlike way, and to let the reader see how I have delved into this subject "by the seat of my pants." For to discuss soulful dreamwork in an academic and analytical way defeats its purpose. I have therefore tried to keep this work close to its source—from whence all dreams come.

And now we begin.

In the Beginning

There is a Hasidic story that tells us that on the night before a soul is placed into the body of a baby about to be born, an angel carries the little soul on its upraised palm up and down the many heavens and worlds. The soul sees everything, and comprehends the mysteries, and knows every thing. It glows with the light of Self knowing. Then, just as the soul is placed in the body of the baby about to be born, the light is extinguished. The infant comes into the world with the rounded indentation at the top and center of its lips—marking the place where the glowing lamp was set. For the rest of its life, the human being hungers for the original sense of well being and knowing connection to God—the glowing light of Self knowing.

Unfortunately, we suffer this loss and alienation from the Self and spend much of our lives searching again for this knowing loving connection.

I AND THOU/THEE AND ME

When Reb Zusya lay dying, he said, "When I approach the pearly gates God will not ask me why I was not more like Moses. No! He will ask why I was not more like Reb Zusya."

We too must become more like Reb Zusya, more one's true self, or "The me that God intended me to be." All those psychoanalytic concepts—Self acceptance, integration, wholeness, meaning, consciousness—are about finding the essential Divine in oneself. It is a way of being authentic, being true to oneself or, one's Self, and it is the real experience of knowing God, intimately. It is the mystic way. It is knowing and merging, both. It has very little to do with "serving" God, and everything to do with love and intention and meaning.

FOLLOWING THE GOLDEN THREAD

I tell you my dreams because a dream is but the story of a dream, yet the story of a dream
is more than a dream—Reb Nachman of Breslov

While we sleep in the dark of the night, the Shekhina extracts the sparks of holiness that have fallen into our dark side. She lovingly returns them to us in dreams and when we remember our dreams we can restore these sparks of holiness, or bits of God to ourselves.

Dreams, dreamwork, and keeping a dream journal become a golden thread that we can follow to find meaning,— to knowing one's Self, or knowing God in one's self. Simply writing down dreams, and allowing them to matter, opens a way. Human beings need meaning, just as we need food and water and air. Without it we suffer dreadful loneliness, alienation, depression, and anxiety. When we begin to pay attention to dreams, a symbol system, a personal mythology, and soul language come into being. We must have what the Jewish mystics call *kavvanah*—serious intention to connect to God and one's Self, to know one's whole Self in a complete and truthful way.

At the end of a long, unhappy marriage a woman dreamt:*

> *I entered a small square white tiled room. It was very cold and clinical. In the corner on*
> *top of a covered toilet sat my husband, naked, and with his knees drawn up, in the position*
> *of the dead. Bodies were left like this in caves at Bet Shean in the Holy land during the*
> *first century. After a year, the flesh came off the bones, and they were put in boxes and*
> *stored deeper in the caves.*
>
> *I reached out and touched my husband. He was neither warm nor cold, neither dead nor*
> *alive. My touch brought him back to life. I thought, this is the last time I can do this.*
>
> *Then I crossed thru a passageway into another small square room bathed in a warm*
> *golden pink light. There, lying on a raised couch or table was the figure of a young girl*
> *on the brink of becoming a woman. She was swathed in a gauzy silken cocoon of pink*
> *gold light.*

---

*All dreams and journal entries are used with the express permission of the dreamers and dream journalists who wish to remain anonymous. None of the dreamers were analysands of mine.

The woman had fallen in love with a man who lived in a distant city on another continent. There was little chance of them ever living together. Each had children and work in their home places that could not be moved. The woman said I knew from the beginning that there was more life in the letters we wrote to each other than there was in my marriage. From the dream I knew that I could not continue in the marriage of death. The pink gold young woman was myself at the age of thirteen or fourteen. That was the time just before my first love. I am being reborn in this new love affair.

Soon after having this dream the woman left her husband. She was finally free to live life fully as herself. Her journey of transformation began.

This Jewish woman joined a group of Sufis who meditated every Thursday night. She usually had a hard time hearing and speaking a foreign language, but in this little group she chanted prayers in Arabic, and seemed to have learned them all by heart the first time she chanted them. There were a few small books written by the teacher of her Sufi group, and she read them. They were very like Chassidic stories. Sufism is the mystical way of Islam, as Chassidism is the mystical way of Judaism. The entire dogma of this particular branch of Sufism was to love God. They would chant the names of God, and ask God to remove the rust from their hearts. Chassidic Jews also, love God, and try to cleave to God, *d'vekut.*

The Path of Love is a Bridge of Hair Over a Chasm of Fire
—A Sufi saying

When she had prayed with the Sufis every Thursday night for six years, never missing a *dzikhr*, the group began to change. The original Sheikh and teacher sent his son-in-law to start a Sufi Center in America.

The woman wrote in her journal:

As Ramadan was ending we looked forward to the Night of Power. That always came on one of the odd numbered nights near the end of Ramadan. It was either the twenty-seventh, twenty-ninth or thirty-first of the month. It was the night that God was in the lowest heaven and closest to earth so all prayers would be heard and answered. That year the thirty-first fell on a Thursday and we were sure that it would be the Night of Power. Even though my practice had dimmed during that year, I was very happy and hopeful as we prepared for dzikhr that night. I arrived at the house where we were to pray early, and waited for dzikhr to begin. Finally, after ten the Sheikh arrived with many of his followers from out of town. He greeted the men in our group with hugs and kisses on both cheeks. Then he began making housing assignments. He said that Abdul Haqq and his family who were arriving from Michigan the next day would stay at my house. I said, "No, my friend Sarah, another lady is staying at my house." Although Sarah was standing right next to me, and I gestured toward her, he ignored me, and went on assigning places.

Finally dzikhr began. After a very short abbreviated dzikhr the Sheikh announced that he would now be collecting money for a Sufi Center in America. He began passing plastic bags around. Then he collected the bags and began counting the money and commenting about the people in California who had given a lot of money, and saying that the women in California had contributed more than the men. He announced our totals, and then invited us to eat. I thought that he'd resume dzikhr after the meal and after the children had eaten and been put to bed. But no, after the meal the Sheikh left, and we all went home.

That night the woman dreamt:

We were doing dzikhr and our Sheikh gave out large heavy New York City telephone directories. The telephone company at that time was distributing these tree wasters every six months. The print was too small for me to see, and I had begun to call people whose number I knew by heart, or from my own Filofax listings. Otherwise, I called Information for a number I did not know. In the dream, however, I thought, if my Sheikh and teacher has given me this, it must have some special meaning and I started to put the one I had received into one of the bookcase niches near me planning to peruse it later. Just then Sheikh said, trade books with someone near you.

The woman wrote in her dream journal:

I woke knowing that this randomly dispensed collective knowledge was of no use to me now, and I would not be praying with the Sufis any longer.

That night she dreamt :

I heard a voice saying, "Why don't you care for the roses at your own home?" Then in the dream I saw a branch of full bodied white roses growing just outside the side door of my house. These roses were actually growing there. I had not planted them and they had never bloomed until that year.

A week later my local newspaper printed a long story about the opening of a Center For Jewish Spirituality and I began to study there.

The roses blooming now, after I have lived here for nearly seven years carry the certainty and the profound weight of synchronicity. I am reassured. I know I am on the right path now.

The woman met her lover in Paris. Each morning as they had breakfast on a market street, she saw large square wooden skids piled high into a cube shape with bread or wine or vegetables. She dreamt:

I saw a cube like the ones we saw each morning and I heard the words: God will provide all that you want and need. I understood even while I was still in the dream that I was expecting more from relationships than they could give me.

The woman remembered the Old Testament injunction to love God with all your heart and soul and with all your might. And then, to love thy neighbor *as* thyself. She understood: Self love, or loving the Divine in one's Self was the source from which all love flowed.

Many years later, the same woman dreamt:

This morning I was dreaming again of trying to make two things work together, or fit, or connect. I had two streams of gold, liquid, or thread. "Tea," I called them. One was White Rose, the other had no name. It was just "the other." The alarm woke me. But hours later, while meditating, the words came to me: "Why don't you care for your roses at home." Suddenly I saw the beautiful white roses on the side of my house and remembered the White Rose tea brand of my childhood. Not the Sufis, not the rabbis, not the institutional, but my own mystic home inside, my roses, my life, steeped, become a golden stream, my dreams: a thread to follow.

A week later, on the eve of the Jewish New Year after dinner with her children and their spouses the woman dreamt of three rolls of gold leaf seen from the side as spirals of golden thread. There was the pink gold as in the cocoon like wrapping of the young woman in her dream of the death marriage that she had at the beginning of her transformative journey, the pure yellow gold of real life, and the violet purple gold of the spirit.

ת   ב   ש

Tav   *Bet*   *Shin*

In the word *Shabbat, shin bet tav,* each Hebrew letter consists of three lines. There is one, the other, and the connection.

Every universe radiates to every other one, and the recipient receives from the giver. But the giver also receives pleasure from the recipient, since its will is done. We are thus taught, "More than the calf wants to suck, the cow wants to suckle" (Talmud *Pesahim* 112a).

The giver is actually both giver and recipient. When a person holds the tension of these two exact opposites and opens himself to the meaning of these words, he understands the reason for the three lines in each of the Hebrew letters in the word *Shabbat.* There is the Giver, the Recipient, and the connection between. Holding the opposites, gives rise to the third way, the way of desire and need, and becomes the intentional, creative, intimate, personal, ecstatic rapture of a mystic experience.

The soul's search for meaning, consciousness, and a deep connection to God is reciprocated by God's need for human beings (The Zohar III, 7b). says that it is we human beings who sustain God in heaven. When a person opens to God, God's will is done, and God delights. As a mystic, a psychologist, a Jungian analyst, I find dreams and dreamwork to be an endlessly rich, frequently ecstatic, source of nourishment and sustenance. It is a way of becoming the best Self one can be, and the one God means one to be.

Seeing and Being "I Am"

Begin with the sh'ma: Listen:

> Sh'ma Yisroael, Adonai, Elohainu, Adonai, Echad.
> Sh'ma, hear, listen, Israel: Adonai, the Lord, Elohainu, Our God,
>   Adonai, Echad, the Lord is One.

This means that there is one God, and that GOD is One, everything, everything and all. God is *Elohim*, a Hebrew word that is both singular *El*, and plural, *Elohim*, both one and many. At first God, *Elohim*, created all from *tohu v'bohu*, chaos and void. That God was both one and the many Gods of that time before time.

Mystics and scholars like Buber, Jung and Isaac Luria believe that God requires man to see God face-to-face so that God can be restored to its original state of ONE, *echad*. The story of Moses and the burning bush perfectly captures this experience of seeing and being seen, and the reciprocal nature of seeing and being. It begins:

> Now Moses kept the flock of Jethro his father-in-law, the priest of
> Midian: and he led the flock to the back side of the desert, and came
> to the mountain of God, even to Horeb (Exodus 3:1).

Moses crosses all the way over to the far side of the wilderness, to Horeb, the mountain of God. He goes to what the Kabbalists call *Aziluth*, or "proximity" in Hebrew. It is a place where God is. The King James Version of the Bible says Moses went to the "back" side of the desert. The Hebrew word translated as back side is *acher*. It is used throughout the Bible to mean "to remain behind, to tarry, to delay." Moses went to the place of tarry, delay, behind—a place of deliberate pause—and then when he is there,

> the angel of the LORD appeared unto him in a flame of fire out of the midst of a bush (Exodus 3:1)

The Bible says literally God himself appeared to Moses in a flame of fire. Immediately, we see the deliberate intentionality of Moses in going there, and the intentionality of God in appearing:

> . . . and he looked, and, behold, the bush burned with fire, and the bush was not consumed (Exodus 3:2).

The word "behold" is *hineh* in Hebrew, which means literally the imperative, "to see here!"

> And Moses said, I will now turn aside, and see this great sight, why the bush is not burnt (Exodus 3:3).

Now, Moses consciously chooses to turn, and turns intentionally in order to see this great sight, this mystery, and understand why the bush is not burnt. He has already seen the burning bush, and he has seen that it burned with fire but was not consumed. Now he wants to see with inner knowing, understanding, the why of this experience. He chooses to seek meaning. He needs to know meaning intimately.

> And when the LORD saw that he turned aside to see, God called unto him out of the midst of the bush, and said, Moses, Moses. And he said, Here am I (Exodus 3:4).

When God sees that Moses has turned aside from his usual way, in order to see, God calls Moses by name, and says Here am I. To be called by name is always personal, always meaningful, and always a harbinger of revelation.

> And he said, Draw not nigh hither: put off thy shoes from off thy feet, for the place whereon thou standest is holy ground (Exodus 3:5).

The great Chassidic Rebbe Moshe of Kobryn says that this means that whenever you turn aside from your usual way, and step out of your usual standpoint—that is, take off your shoes—you make a connection with the sacred and holy ground.

Then God says an amazing thing: "*I am the God of thy father . . .*"

This is the only time in the Bible that God says to anyone "I am the God of your own personal father." Something unusual is about to happen here.

> And Moses hid his face; for he was afraid to look upon God (Exodus 3:6).

Later, God does appear to Moses face to face, but for now let us listen to the conversation that follows.

> And the LORD said, I have surely seen the affliction of my people which are in Egypt, and have heard their cry by reason of their taskmasters; for I know their sorrows; And I am come down to deliver them out of the hand of the Egyptians, and to bring them up out of that land unto a good land and a large, unto a land flowing with milk and honey (Exodus 3:7-8).

God says that he has *surely seen* the affliction of the people, and has *heard their cry* and has come to deliver them out of Egypt, *mizriam*, which in Hebrew means the narrow place. Emotionally, and psychologically the narrow place is the powerful constricting negative hold of one's complexes and fears.

Then God says he wants Moses to go to Pharaoh and convince him to let the enslaved people go.

> And Moses said unto God, Who am I, that I should go unto Pharaoh, and that I should bring forth the children of Israel out of Egypt? (Exodus 3:11).

Moses demurs, asking, Who am I? How can I possibly accomplish this huge task of facing the powerful despotic hold of the narrow materialistic way of Egypt with it its many Gods and hierarchical pyramidal structure, and with the god-like all powerful Pharaoh at the top?

God explains that he will be with Moses, that this presence is a token, a sign, and a certain proof that Moses can do what is being asked of him. Here is the amazing reciprocal relationship. God needs Moses to free the people, and Moses needs God *with him* in order to accomplish what he is called to do.

~~~

A woman writer who had recently authored a controversial book, dreamt:

All the little children, part of a cult, were to be killed. They were trapped in a room. I am in the room in order to try to save them. I called them to me, wordlessly, gesturing, ssh-hhusssshing them to be quiet. Suddenly a trap door opened in the floor and Amish women began coming up from below. I thought, "All I can do now is use my words to speak to them, and that will save the little children."

The dreamer had authored several academic, well documented, histori-cal biographies. She knew nothing about Amish women except that they were restricted and caught in tradition and rules, but she could speak to them with words, and thereby save the children. I suggested to her that the Amish women, were "I am" parts of herself. These "I-am" female elements were beginning to rise up in her. By speaking face to face to the repressed, restricted, caught-in-the-past womanly parts of herself. she would become more truly her authentic Self—"I am."

~~~

The Bible story of Moses and God continues with God saying,

Certainly I will be with thee; and this shall be a token unto thee, that I have sent thee: When thou hast brought forth the people out of Egypt, ye shall serve God upon this mountain (Exodus 3:12).

Moses, still doubtful, asks again for God to clarify its meaning:

And Moses said unto God, Behold, when I come unto the children of Israel, and shall say unto them, The God of your fathers hath sent me unto you; and they shall say to me, What is his name? what shall I say unto them? (Exodus 3:13).

And God, Elohim the plural and singular God now becomes the name Ehayeh, which means "be, become,"—"I am"!

And God said unto Moses, I AM THAT I AM: and he said, Thus shalt thou say unto the children of Israel, I AM hath sent me unto you. And God said moreover unto Moses, Thus shalt thou say unto the children of Israel, The LORD God of your fathers, the God of Abraham, the God of Isaac, and the God of Jacob, hath sent me unto you: this is my name for ever, and this is my memorial unto all generations (Exodus 3:14-15).

This is the basic paradigm: God, *Elohim*, the one God *El*, and the plural, *Elohim*, or many, needs man in order to become "I am." Then *Ehayeh* (which means literally "be," "become"), God, says to Moses, "Tell the people that I Am —*Yud Heh Vav Heh*—— the same word in the nominal form— has sent you." Yud Heh Vav Heh is the secret ineffable name of God. It is pronounced Yahweh, *Adonai*, or not at all. The Jews and Samaritans did not say this name for God at all. They used the word *ha-Shem*, meaning the Name. *Yud Heh Vav Heh* is a form of the Hebrew word for "life" and means the one bringing into being or existence, life giver, creator, performer of promises, and he who causes lightning and rain, and even enemies to fall.

In this encounter with Moses God becomes I Am, the one who is, the absolute, existing, ever living, ever coming into manifestation, self consistent, unchangeable one. *Yud, Heh, Vav, Heh*, is the God who revealed himself to Moses at Horeb and who is with Moses in his great endeavor to free his people from slavery.

יהוה

When man knows God in the way Moses and God encounter each other, then man aids in the work of continuous creation. The *Chassidim* call this *d'vekut*, or cleaving to God in order to be as fully, responsibly, consciously, authentically oneself as one can be. This is a relationship to Self, or God that is beyond ego. It is the *imago dei*. It is was is meant by "*So God created man in his own image, in the image of God created he him*" (Genesis 1:27). It is an inner experience of God, as one's true authentic Self. Jung calls this the Self, and Abulafia, the thirteenth-century Jewish mystic, calls it the Active Intellect. This is not the personal ego of me, or myself. It is the indwelling experience of God, the *Shekhina*, from which the ego is born in a process of psychic mitosis while a person is still in the womb. It is that to which the prophet Isaiah refers when he says,

> Yahweh called me before I was born, from my mother's womb he pronounced my name (Isaiah 49:1).

Then there is Moses, a human being, heroically seeking consciousness and meaning. On the far side of the wilderness, Moses sees something numinous. He sees, he turns from the path, removes his shoes and asks, who are you? And God says, *Ehayeh*, I am that I am. When Moses sees God, or *because* Moses sees God, God becomes wholly "I Am," and says "I see, and I hear the suffering of my people. Take your people from the narrow confines of slavery in Egypt."

KNOWING GOD

Moses set out to do God's bidding and free the people from slavery. God had already made nine plagues fall upon Egypt, when finally Pharaoh said to Moses,

> Get thee from me, take heed to thyself, see my face no more; for in that day thou seest my face thou shalt die. And Moses said, Thou hast spoken well, I will see thy face again no more (Exodus 10:28-29).

Although Pharaoh has already told Moses to go, God says to Moses,

> Yet will I bring one plague more upon Pharaoh, and upon Egypt; afterwards he will let you go hence: when he shall let you go, he shall

surely thrust you out hence altogether. Speak now in the ears of the people, and let every man borrow of his neighbour, and every woman of her neighbour, jewels of silver, and jewels of gold (Exodus 11:1-2).

This instruction always seemed very odd to me. The urgency and seeming secrecy of "Speak now in the ears of the people" caught my attention. Why did the children of Israel need the gold and silver of the Egyptians?

God brought the last plague against the first born sons of Egypt,. . . And the people took their dough before it was leavened, their kneading troughs being bound up in their clothes upon their shoulders. And the children of Israel did according to the word of Moses; and they borrowed of the Egyptians jewels of silver, and jewels of gold, and raiment: And the LORD gave the people favour in the sight of the Egyptians, so that they lent unto them such things as they required (Exodus 12:34-36).

So the Israelites left Egypt with their lives, their unleavened bread, their kneading troughs and the gold and silver and the raiment of the Egyptians. Soon afterward, Pharaoh ordered his army to pursue the Israelites and they drove them to banks of the Red Sea. Whereupon God made the Red Sea part, and when the Israelites had crossed over to the other side, and Pharaoh's army was in the middle of the sea, the waters closed over them. Many *midrashim* say that God rode a mare, and the excited stallions of the Pharaoh's army pursued the beloved mare into the sea where they drowned. And so again, according to *midrash,** more of the bounty of the Egyptians' gold and silver adornments fell to the Israelites.

For many years I wondered about this gold and silver that was both given to the Israelites, and taken from the Egyptians. The gold and silver seem to

---

* A *midrash* is a search born of an apparent hole or inconsistency or mystery in scripture. Midrash is a way of interpreting biblical stories that goes beyond simple meaning. A midrash is a story that explains a mystery, something that has not been explained in scripture.

be on a par with the daily bread. Then suddenly, when I was writing a book about amulets, talismans, and magical jewelry, it occurred to me that the gold and silver, jewels and raiment, that the Israelites took with them from Egypt was the personal mystical experience of knowing God *inside*, and as basic as daily bread. It is the soulful inner way of Kabbalah and alchemy with their symbolic meanings of gold and silver as transcendent psychological values.

A woman told me her dream, saying,

I remember the first dream I had when I began analysis: I was walking through mud, a muddy river, or a river of mud and I bent down and pulled from the mud a gold rope with my right hand, and a silver rope in my left hand. I was, somehow, to weave them together.

At that time in her life she needed to use the strong ropelike connections of both the solar gold and lunar silver to do the analytic work of knowing herself, or her Self.

Later, in the story of Exodus, when Moses was on the mountain of God for too long, the people felt frightened and abandoned. They misused these inner ways of knowing God, or perhaps they had not yet learned it. They made the gold and silver into a golden calf and worshipped it as God.

The Talmud says that Abraham had received occult knowledge or Kabbalah from Melchizedec the king of Salem. Or, it is said, even earlier, the angel Raziel gave a book of secret knowledge to Adam on his first night after being exiled from the garden of Eden. Adam passed it to Noah, from whom it descended to Abraham, who then gave these gifts of esoteric knowledge to his Egyptian concubine, Keturah. She passed these secrets on to her sons, who were also the sons of Abraham and who traveled as missionaries to Egypt and taught the mysteries to the Egyptians. Perhaps the Israelites' stay in Egypt—outside the holy land, surrounded and tyrannized by others, and forbidden to practice their religion outwardly,—became a retort within which the people began to experience God inside themselves.

God instructed the Israelites to take this esoteric wisdom away with them when they left Egypt, but their years of separation and slavery had taken a heavy toll, and they obviously had not yet understood completely and reliably how to use this inner way of knowing God when they made the golden calf. They faltered and lost their way, as we all do from time to time. The Baal Shem Tov, the master of the good name and founder of Chassidism, advises that when people sin it is because the *Yetzer-ha-Ra*, the Evil Impulse, has misled led them, and it wants them to be frightened and depressed and *not* worship God. Knowing this—and recognizing that making a mistake, feeling depressed, being despondent and lost is a natural part of being human—frees one to reconnect with God and continue on the path of loving God, and being loved.

Kabbalah means, *received* tradition. It is both a *received* traditional way of knowing God, and a way of *receiving* God inside oneself by being receptive, meditative, open and listening. One can enter into an act of continuous creation, and make God whole again as it was originally in the time before time. The Zohar speaks of "The world that is coming..." as both a messianic era to come, and the real and actual world of now that is continually coming and becoming. Both man and God are engaged in this process. Psychologically, this is the dynamic work of analysis and individuation: gathering the sparks of consciousness, withdrawing what we project onto others and integrating it back into oneself, opening a continual dialogue between the ego, and the Self, or, as Buber puts it, between I and Thou. This dialogue is easily seen and felt in dreams and soulful dreamwork

Dreams of Love

The Song of Songs is a long, lyrical, sensual and erotic love poem. It is an entire book of the Bible that never once mentions God. It is a complete book of love. It speaks of kisses sweeter than wine, and breasts like fawns, and clusters of grapes, a belly like a heap of wheat surrounded by lilies, the lover's thighs as pillars of marble, his belly of ivory, of love being stronger than death, and of the incredible overweening need of human beings for the healing *coniunctio* of love, both human and divine.

During the Rabbinical synod at Jabneh in the early part of the second century there was much discussion of whether or not the Song of Songs should be included in the Bible at all. Rabbi Akiva finally held sway saying, the whole world attained its supreme value on the day the Song of Songs was given to the children of Israel. He added that all the scriptures are holy, but the Song of Songs is the Holy of Holies. Had the Torah, the great book of Jewish law, not been given, the Song of Songs would have sufficed to guide the world.

The Holy of Holies, the ark of the covenant, is surmounted by two Cherubim with their wings outstretched and touching. The wings are described as more than merely touching. They are said to be cleaving to each other, and intertwined. The wings of the cherubim form a *chuppah* or marriage canopy over the Holy of Holies and the Throne of God. The Shekhina—the indwelling feminine aspect of God—dwells in the Holy of Holies. The word Cherubim contains the same three Hebrew letters as the word for blessing, and the Hebrew word for grafting in order to create new life. Jewish mystics would therefore say that the three things—the intertwined cherubim, the blessing, and the new creation that grows from the intentional connecting of one to another—share a root meaning.

And thou shalt make two cherubim of gold, of beaten work shalt thou make them, in the two ends of the mercy seat. And make one cherub on the one end, and the other cherub on the other end: even of the mercy seat shall ye make the cherubim on the two ends thereof. And the cherubim shall stretch forth their wings on high, covering the mercy seat with their wings, and their faces shall look one to another; toward the mercy seat shall the faces of the cherubim be. And thou shalt put the mercy seat above upon the ark; and in the ark thou shalt put the testimony that I shall give thee. And there I will meet with thee, and I will commune with thee from above the mercy seat, from between the two cherubim which are upon the ark of the testimony (Exodus 25:18-23).

Here is the promise that God will commune with his children from the Holy of Holies, from his Throne of Glory under the wings of the Cherubim.

And the priests brought in the ark of the covenant of the LORD unto his place, into the oracle of the house, to the holy of holies, even under the wings of the cherubim. For the cherubim spread forth their two wings over the place of the ark, and the cherubim covered the ark (I Kings 8:6-8; 2 Chronicles 5:7-9).

And it came to pass, when the priests were come out of the holy place, that the cloud filled the house of the LORD, So that the priests could not stand to minister because of the cloud: for the glory of the LORD had filled the house of the LORD.

Then spake Solomon, The LORD said that he would dwell in the thick darkness. I have surely built thee an house to dwell in, a settled place for thee to abide in for ever (I Kings 10-14).

We are God. God is each one of us. The one we long for and need and want is the Self, or the significant spark of God inside us, the Self we always were and were intended to be. Indeed, the Song of Songs perfectly expresses

God's love for human beings, and our love for God, as well as the divine spark in our human love for each other. The Song of Songs is a compendium of all the many ways of love and a complete guide for being human.

In the beginning, when God created the heaven and the earth, and separated the darkness from the light, and the heavens from the waters and the land, and created the vegetation, and the great lights, and the flying fowl, and the great sea monsters and creeping creatures and beasts of the earth, he simply *did* it (Genesis 1:1-26). However, when it came to the creation of human beings, God said first, with due deliberation, and the magisterial *we*,

Let us make man in our image, after our likeness (Genesis 1:26).

And then, after stating this intention,

God created man in His own image, in the image of God created He him; male and female created He them (Genesis 1:27).

There was real intention here. A plan, and a plan carried out.

A young woman plagued by self doubt always felt that she was not "enough" for her mother. She told me she had always wondered whether "God created man in his own image" meant that she was like God and simply "being herself" was "enough," or whether God created man in his own image meant that God had an image of perfection that she needed to be in order to be loved.

As a grown woman and a mother herself she dreamt:

I am sitting on the lap of my first boyfriend. His arms are around me and he loves me completely. I feel loved and love him completely. He is an Angel.

Now I understand. He was an Angel of God, and that embrace is inside me. I do not have to be anything but my Self, to be loved.

The second word of the Old Testament is *barah*. It means create, but it is only used to describe creation which has a divine element. We say "making love" when we speak of sexual acts performed with love. There are times when we feel that, indeed, we have created love, made love, not merely to have expressed love, but actually to have created love just as God has created.

God has created male and female, in His own image . . . In his own image he created them. Nevertheless, each of us does lose the connection to our own soul and to the Self within. This happens to some at birth, and to some in infancy or childhood. It is then that we feel fully and completely alone, on our own, small, cold, sad, lonely, and frightened. It seems to be a natural consequence of being dependent upon imperfect parents and fate, and it is exacerbated in later life when one tries to restore the original wholeness and soul connection in a relationship.

To begin with, the soul is lovingly projected onto the beloved. Soon, unfortunately, the beloved does not live up to the projection, or disappoints, or disappears, or any of the other disasters that befall the human heart. In a series of soft compromises, unnoticed, unknowingly, one has lost the connection to what one really wants and needs. The connection with one's own soul is lost. The heart is broken, but this break is an opening and a beginning. There is nothing so whole as a broken heart, says an old Yiddish proverb.

The Song of Songs is about the struggle to form that inner soulful connection and all the vicissitudes of that great adventure. According to the Zohar, The Book of Splendor of the Kabbalists, Solomon composed the Song of Songs on the same day that the first temple was completed in Jerusalem. At the heart of the temple is the Holy of Holies where the Shekhina, the Divine Presence, dwells. The Shekhina is that loving personal connection to the divine we experience when we study Torah for its own sake, pray, or meditate, or love. The Kabbalists speak of the Shekhina as God's beloved, the Queen, the Matrona, the feminine side of God. The Talmud and the prophets speak of the people of Israel as God's beloved. *Shabbat,* the Sabbath, is also God's bride. As the daughter and granddaughter of eminent rabbis have explained, "Everything in nature is paired in order to create and reproduce. So when God made the days, Sunday had Monday, and Tuesday had Wednesday, and Thursday had Friday, but Saturday had no partner, so God took *Shabbat* to be his bride."

Martin Buber calls this dialogue between man and God "the greatest of all values,"

> ... the reciprocal relationship between the human and the divine, the reality of the I and the You which does not cease at the rim of eternity. ... If you direct the undiminished power of your fervor to God's world destiny, if you do what you must do at this moment— no matter what it might be!—with your whole strength and with kavanah, with holy intent, you will bring about the union between God and Shekhina, eternity and time... Do not rebel against your desires, but seize them and bind them to God (*Tales of the Hasidim, Early Masters*, p. 6).

The entire Song of Songs attests to this notion of God and Shekhina. It is the love poem of God and man. The Talmud says, he who recites any of the verses of the Song of Songs at a feast, making of it merely a kind of wine song, brings evil into the world and has no place in the world to come. However, if one takes the sensual human feelings and natural poetic images of the Song to heart, the experience is of a glorious wholeness, a joyous earthly paradise, a *coniunctio* of the human and divine spirit.

> *The Song of Songs resembles locks to which the keys have been lost.*
> —*The Saadia Gaon*

During the eleventh century, Rashi wrote a lengthy allegorical interpretation of the Song of Songs. He says that Solomon foresaw that the people of Israel would be carried into one exile after another, and in their suffering they would remember their former glory and the love that God had bestowed upon them. Rashi believed that Solomon produced the Song of Songs by divine inspiration, speaking as a woman who feels herself to be the widow of a living husband and longing for her lost love. Her husband, moved by her sorrow, remembers her loyalty, her beauty, and her good works which had bound him to her in everlasting love.

Rashi tried to show that God did not afflict his beloved bride, the people of Israel, or human beings, willingly. Although he did put her away, he has not cast her off. She is still his wife and he is still her husband and will return to her. Thus, paraphrasing Rashi, one might say people chosen or choosing a path of self realization and psychological individuation will experience alienation, exile, and despair while on the way. Love, memory of love, and hope can sustain one while on the road.

The experience of having been loved or happy in some young and far off time, before, and then, now, feeling cast out and abandoned is all too familiar. This memory of having been happy and whole long ago is the subject of Wordsworth's poem, *Ode: Intimations of Immortality from Recollections of Early Childhood.* The feeling of having lost one's way, and feeling alien, lonely and desolate is a result of having become fragmented and separated from an original wholeness and knowing connection to God as Self. The sense of loss and abandonment is endemic to the human condition.

A man of seventy dreamt that he was becoming platinum, or, returning to being platinum which was his original state. He felt home again as he had been at his beginning. A few days later he decided to adopt an old dog, in order, he said, to heal the fear in his heart. He had remembered that his grandfather had suddenly and brutally shot his beloved dog when the man and the dog were both thirteen. The dog had done something, perhaps as a result of being old, that had angered the grandfather. It was the first bad thing that the dreamer had seen done intentionally. His mother had died when the man was six and, while he might have felt sorrow and loss then, he said, the brutality of his grandfather killing the dog had put fear in his heart from that time on. After that, love was always framed by fear. The dream of becoming platinum again resulted in his poem:

> *First Things*
> *A platinum gauze, finer than spider's silk*
> *No, finer even than rays of physical light*
> *Suffused my mind; it was*
> *The light of mind stuff,*
> *Unpolluted by earthly images.*

It dissolved into my being as a child,
No, not my being, my physical being,
But my child's spirit and,
No, not a child—that was already
later;
It was the uniqueness that I came
into the world with.
Platinum, unsustainable, indestructible,
Empty—vacant but uniquely Me.
I was home at last, the course well run,
The world dropping away like an
Early morning dream
Nowhere to go.

BODY AND SOUL

The explicit sexual language of the Song of Songs is very like Ezekiel's description of God's love for Israel,

> Your breasts were already formed and your hair was grown. . . And behold your time was a time of love; and I spread my skirt over you and covered your nakedness . . . and you became mine (Ezekiel 16:7-9).

The purely physical and sensual imagery of the Song of Songs is seductive, compelling, achingly and astonishingly familiar. Each of us must bring the human, the instinctual, the animal, and the divine elements of being into knowing connection. Martin Buber tells us that only when the soul is within the physical body, working through its limbs, can the soul reach perfection. The soul itself is not more holy than the body, and the body cannot exist without the soul; when the soul leaves, the flesh falls into decay.

Celebrate the joy, and pleasure of human erotic love, as one loves God:

> Why was King David immediately forgiven for the sin of killing Uriah the Hittite and husband of Bathsheba? Because David desired

God's forgiveness with the same passionate desire that he had for Bathsheba (The Rizhiner Rebbe).

Ibn Ezra gives a complete allegorical interpretation of the Song of Songs telling the love story of a girl who falls in love with a shepherd, and a king who tries to separate the lovers, while the young woman remains true to her love for the shepherd. Rashi, Rashbam and Ibn Ezra are moved, like Solomon to speak in the woman's voice of love lost. Whether virgin, bride, lover or widow, separation from the beloved is the cause of the Song, and re-membering their loving union is its content and purpose.

Scholars offer a rational allegorical approach to the Song of Songs, while mystics, Jewish, Christian and Muslim go more passionately and directly to the heart of the matter. Sufis love God. There is no other element of dogma in their religion. Their word for worship, *dzikhr*, means re-membrance. Sufi's chant the names of God, pray for God to remove the rust from their hearts, and long to become one with God. Rabia, a Sufi woman saint, when asked if she hated the devil, said, "My love for God leaves no room in my heart for anything else." Hasidic Jews also long for *d'vekut*, a way of cleaving to God, or becoming one with God. They practice the commandments with love, not fear, because separation from God hurts.

Christian mystics, like St. John of the Cross wrote,

All things of the maker
forgotten—but not Him
exploration within,
and loving the Lover.
        ("Peak of Perfection")

Mirabai, a Hindu devotee of Krishna writes,

Beloved!
I wander still
In quest of You!
I am athirst

For your Eternal Love
I long to make
My body a lamp—
The wick whereof will be
My tender heart.
    ("In Quest of You")
Within me throbs the ache
of longing and love for You.
    ("My Heart is Athirst")

As above, so below.
Know this and rejoice.
    (Alchemical and Kabalistic recipe)

While mystics, Sufis, Chassid's, and Christians have expressed their longing for a loving connection with the divine in poetry and prayer throughout the ages, nowhere are these feelings so overtly physical, sexual, and human as in the Song of Songs. The Song of Songs is the only book of the Bible that does not mention God at all. It speaks only of the love and longing of one human being body for another. Certainly it can be heard as a lyrical, archetypal outpouring of longing for the lost soul mate, the other half of oneself, "...the comrade/twin whose palm/would bear a lifeline like our own" (Adrienne Rich, "Natural Resources," *The Dream of a Common Language*, 62)

A woman in love dreamt:

I am in bed with my lover. We lie side by side. There is another body neither male nor female that is across and above our heads. It forms us into the Hebrew letter heh—*the most essential economical name for God.*

ה

Human beings are said to have been "created male and female in God's own image, he created them" (Genesis 1:27). Several lines later in Genesis one reads, "It is not good for Adam, *Adom* the red earth human being to be alone," all one, at one, so God opened up one side, or some say, sawed the human being apart from its back, and created the other destined to be Eve or *Chava*, mother of all who live (Genesis 2:21-22). Then there were two. One and an other. No longer one, nor fixed back to back, but free to be face to face, side by side, or each one alone, and apart.

There are many *midrashim* or stories about this primal separation. Sometimes a *midrash* is a story that grows up in the crack between this and that. *Midrashim* are often felt as revelations or holy connections. Dreamwork or the active imagination that seeks meaning from one's dreams is a form of *midrash*. The mystery of the disappearance of the original female created of red earth like Adam gave rise to the *midrash* that, because of their common origins, she felt equal to him and therefore she refused to lie beneath him in sexual intercourse. When he threatened to overpower her she uttered the ineffable name of God, and flew away to the Red Sea to consort with demons. The name of the original female is Lilith; her name is derived from her ability to fly. *Lil* is the Sumerian name for a storm demon. It was later confabulated with *lilah* the Hebrew word for night. Thus, the original woman became Lilith a night flying female demon.

Adam longed for her return, but she refused, so God made Adam fall into a deep sleep and created Eve from his rib. After Adam and Eve sinned by eating from the tree of knowledge, Adam withdrew from sexual relations with Eve and wore a belt of thorny twigs around his waist. Into this separation Lilith returned and mounted him, taking her pleasure with him and flying away. She is said to return evermore, causing erotic dreams and nocturnal emissions in men who sleep alone, and killing the babies of the daughters of Eve who do not properly acknowledge her rightful presence.

According to the Zohar, The Book of Splendor of the Kabbalists, when the people of Israel sinned, God was separated from the Matrona, and instead, took Lilith the handmaiden to be his consort. Lilith is called the lower Shekhina, and the Matrona is the higher Shekhina. The two are joined when men and women make love. When human beings make love in full recognition of the divine presence including the original female, Lilith,

God and the Shekhina are reunited in loving embrace and the *seraphim* sing the Song of Songs.

Chassid's believe that all of creation is evidence of God, and love of God is continuous creation. The Gnostics too, say that originally there was only one being, and at first thought the soul descended. Evermore, there is a sense of longing for a soul mate, and a terrible sense of primordial separation from an original wholeness or oneness of male and female, as well as an original oneness with God. Thus, the Song of Songs may be heard as the symphony of creation and a cry of love and longing of male for female, and female for male, in order that their soul mating may restore their original divine wholeness and oneness.

> *Where have you hidden away?*
> *You left me whimpering, my love.*
> *Wounding me you vanished*
> *like the stag. I rushed out*
> *Shouting for you—but you were gone.*
> (Spiritual Canticle, St. John the Divine)

Whether one understands the Song of Songs as allegorical, mystical, or simply literal, the clear meaning of the book is that love, the knowing connection, besides being the strongest emotion in the human heart, is also the holiest. Dreams are, I believe, a manifestation of this need. Soulful integration of dreamwork is a way of making this inner *coniunctio* and healing both the terrible dis-ease and split between body and soul, and the painful sense of loss and longing for love, both human and divine.

The World of Emanation

Isaac Luria (1534–1572), Jewish mystic and rabbi, is considered the father of contemporary Kabbalah. He was called the Ari, or Lion. The initial letters of his name, Rabbi Isaac Ashkenazi, were permutated to the Ari, or the Holy Lion (*aryeh* means lion in Hebrew). The Ari was born in Jerusalem, where his family had emigrated from Germany (hence we find the term "Ashkenazi" for descendants of Eastern Europe.) After his father died, his mother took him to Egypt where he grew up in the house of his wealthy uncle. He spent much of his time alone on an island in the Nile near Cairo, where he studied the Zohar and other Kabbalistic works. The Ari came to Safed, a hill town in northern Palestine, from Egypt in the sixteenth century. He was a Jewish mystic and cosmologist. The synagogue of the Ari is a tiny blue and white building with a domed roof. There is a simple wooden podium a few steps off the floor in the center of the room. The synagogue is hidden and tucked away in the midst of the village. Cats lie in the sun in the little garden in front. It is the most peaceful place I have ever been. The Ari died before he was forty. He wrote little, and told his ideas to only a few of his closest associates. Nevertheless, his understanding of the original creation and the mystic way spread to the far corners of the earth.

The Ari taught that before God as we know it, before time and the world began, there was *Ein-Sof. Ein-Sof* means "no thing"—without end, a formless primordial nothingness. It is best described by what it is not. *Ein-Sof* the God of the Kabbalah, is without qualities or intentionality or boundaries. It is God the Immanent, and the Absolute All. It was called by the early Spanish Kabbalists "Root of Roots," and "Great Reality," or "Indifferent Unity." *Ein-Sof*—nothingness—was everywhere and every thing.

Ein-Sof has no attributes because they can manifest only within existence and existence is finite. The oral tradition of Kabbalah says that the reason for existence is that God wished to behold God. According to the Zohar, the thirteenth century Book of Splendor of the Kabbalists, before there was balance or universe ". . . face did not gaze upon face." Thus, the first chapter of Genesis is the unfolding of an already existing divine world. The first words of the Old testament, "In the beginning God created," are more properly, and more grammatically stated as, "In the beginning of creating..."

In an act of total free will God withdrew *Ein-Sof*, the Absolute All, from one place to allow a void in no-thing in which the mirror of being could manifest. In order to create the world, God had to make a space within itself by contracting into and away from itself. Isaac Luria called this divine contraction, *tzimtzum*.

Ein-Sof emanated a beam of light that penetrated from the periphery toward the center and manifested in a lightning flash of ten emanations called the ten *Sefirot*. *Sefira*, the singular of the word, has no simple equivalent in any language. Its root is related to "cipher" or number, and to "sapphire." The Sefirot are visualized as *kelim*, Holy Vessels containing the divine attributes.

The patriarch Abraham had a revelation which he recorded in Sefer Yetzirah, the Book of Creation. He described the Sefirot in all their fantastic, dynamic dreamlike intensity

> The *Sefirot* are all one: they are measured by ten without end, the depth of the first and the depth of the last, the depth of good and the depth of evil, the depth of above and the depth below, the depth of the east and the depth of the west, the depth of the north and the depth of the south. One Lord, God the faithful King, rules them all from His Holy dwelling for all eternity. . . . Their appearance is like a flash of lightning and their destination is beyond bounds. His word is in them when they go out and when they return. At his command

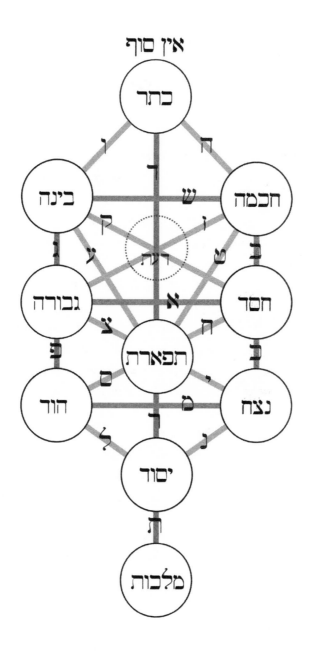

they rush like a whirlwind and bow down before his throne . . . their end is linked to their beginning and their beginning to their end, as the flame is linked to the burning coal. Know, think, and visualize that the Lord is one without second . . . restrains your mouth from speaking and your heart from thinking. And if your mouth races to speak and your heart to think, return to the place about which it is written: "And the living creatures rushed out and returned." (*Sefer Yetzirah*, Irving Friedman, Trans., 1977).

The Sefirot, each carrying an unerasable name for God, are arranged in a series of triangles with the top Sefira being *Keter* or Crown and named Eheyeh and the bottom most vessel which contains the Shekhina being *Malcuth* or Kingdom and named Adonai. Beneath the crown are the *Sefirot* of *Hokhmah*, Wisdom named Yah, *Binah*, Understanding named YHVH with the vowels of Elohim, *Chesed* or Love named El, *Gevurah*, Strength named Elohim, *Tiferet*, Beauty named YHVH, *Netsah*, Eternity named Tsva'ot, and *Yesod*, Foundation named Shaddai.

These *Sefirot* form the Kabbalistic Tree of Life and Death, a three dimensional dynamic diagrammatic form consisting of three triads of vessels, arranged as three pillars, with a crown and a base, and pathways between. The upper and middle triad of vessels were able to contain the light of *Ein-Sof*, but the vessels of the lowest triad were mixed with a fearful regressive holding back energy and were too fragile to contain the light.

There was a terrible catastrophe. The vessels of the lowest triad shattered and the Holy Sparks of *Ein-Sof*, the *Nitzotzot*, or points of light, flew in all directions. Some returned to its infinite source, but many more fell into primordial space, and became covered with evil husks or shells called *klippot*. These Holy Sparks of *Ein-Sof*, weighted down with their husks, entered into all things in the World of Form which includes mankind. With the shattering of the vessels, man, like God, was made to contain both good and evil. The divine sparks are scattered everywhere and long to return to the divine wholeness but cannot, because they are trapped in the *klippot* and material existence.

Isaac Luria believed that it was the sacred and redemptive responsibility of mankind to gather the Holy Sparks of consciousness and meaning, and thereby restore *Ein-Sof* or God to wholeness. This work of repair is called *tikkun ha olam*, the work of repairing the world. I believe that soulful dreamwork analysis, and seeking meaning are an in-gathering of these divine sparks in order to restore a loving connection to God or the Self.

PART TWO

Soulful Dreamwork

Dreams

In a dream, in a vision of the night when deep sleep falls upon men, in slumberings upon the bed, then he opens the ears of men and seals their instruction (Job 33:15-16).

A dream not interpreted is like a letter unread . . .
(Chisda, Talmud Berakoth, 87)

The ancients understood that dreams are divinely inspired. They arise from the divine spark present in each of us. Any concentrated attention to one's dreams begins a dialectical process that feels good, restores one to oneself, and has unexpected and far reaching beneficial effects. Even the simple act of remembering or retelling or recording a dream has a restorative effect. The meaning of re-membering, or re-collecting is better expressed when there is a hyphen to connect the dismembered parts. Like the Kabbalist, Isaac Luria, I believe that originally *Ein-Sof* became Sefirot, vessels that contained all of God's attributes. The vessels shattered and the divine sparks flew into the world. Recollecting dreams is the work of restoring the Sefirot and the Self within.

When Self is written with a capital S it refers to that experience of the divine within oneself. There is a way of Self-knowledge or Self-realization wherein all the disparate, despised, and desired elements in a dream are redeemed from their exile, and ingathered by the eye of love. The dream must be welcomed with an open and listening heart, and viewed with loving acceptance.

Integration is the essential, basic, and overweening principle of soulful dreamwork. The mechanics of the process are simple. If the dreamer appears in the dream, he or she carries the conscious ego attitude of the person dreaming. The same-sexed people in the dream carry the shadow, or dissociated, unwanted, disliked, despised, or sometimes, as-yet-unlived positive qualities of the dreamer. The opposite sexed people carry the contra-sexual and often times soulful qualities the dreamer seeks, and sometimes, fears. Animals, children, and babies, too, carry soulful spiritual qualities. The setting, plot, and atmosphere of the dream is a highly creative representation of the dreamer's psychic situation. All meaning is conveyed in the dream by image, word, and deed. Often, in addition to the historic precedents, and current state, there is a further prophetic meaning to the dream.

> A people who do not dream never attain to inner sincerity, for only in his dreams is a man really himself. Only for his dreams is a man responsible—his actions are what he must do. Actions are a bastard race to which a man has not given his full paternity (A letter from J.B. Yeats to his son W.B. Yeats, August 30, 1914).

Jewish wisdom likens Torah study to a polished mirror. The closer one approaches, the closer one is approached. Similarly, the face one turns toward the unconscious, and to one's dreams, is the face it turns toward you. The dreamer, by a process of active imagination can discover the personal meaning of each of the dream elements.

Active imagination is not free association. In many ways it is opposite to free association. It is a practice whereby the courageous dreamer dreams the dream onward. He asks the various people and elements in the dream to communicate with each other and sometimes with him. When this is done in a spirit of truth and loving open receptivity there is much to be learned. One is often surprised. This process done truthfully tells you something you did not already know. If one understands a dream, or reads it as a sacred text, as divine instruction, it brings insight, illumination, recognition, and a certain sense of joy in being restored. Indeed, one gains a miraculous sense of healing and wholeness by accepting one's own dream as a psychological phenomenon in which all the elements of the dream are parts of oneself. The bastard spawn becomes the beloved child.

The Kabbalists believe that while we sleep in the dark of the night, the Shekhina extracts the sparks of holiness that have fallen into our dark side. She lovingly returns them to us in dreams and when we re-member our dreams we can restore these sparks of holiness, or bits of God to ourselves

THE INDWELLING SHEKHINA

They shall make a sanctuary for Me, so that I may dwell among them ... (Exodus 25:8).

The Biblical commandment to make a sanctuary so that "I may dwell among you" literally means that there is an indwelling divine presence in each and every one of us. The commandment to construct a tabernacle can be taken personally.. Each of us is a living tabernacle. The Hebrew root of the word Shekhina, shin, khaf, nun means dwell, abide, settle down, remain, encamp, and settle permanently. In Syriac, Arabic, and Assyrian and all the languages of the ancient Middle East this word connotes a state of being: settling down, at rest, in peace and dwelling in security.

I have spoken of the Shekhina as the feminine side of God, but Shekhina should be thought of as "the indwelling divine." God is One, and the Shekhina is the human experience of God dwelling within oneself. It carries all the connotative meaning of being at peace and secure. The Rambam (Moses Maimonides), when writing about Jacob, likens the departure of the Shekhina to a period of terrible melancholy, lethargy, and anxiety. During all the days of his mourning for his son Joseph, Jacob suffered sorrow and anxiety. The holy spirit, the Shekhina, departed from him. When Jacob was told that Joseph was alive, the Targum says, the spirit of Jacob revived and the spirit of prophesy again rested upon him. The Divine Presence is experienced as inward joy.

The Shekhina, the Divine Presence, dwells primarily in the human heart. The Zohar compares every person to the Temple, the permanent Tabernacle.

Just as the center of the Temple is the Holy of Holies, the center of the human being is his heart. The holiness that is the source of all that is good in the world emanates from the Holy of Holies, and the life force of a human being emanates from the heart.

The parallels go deeper. The Holy of Holies houses the Ark of the Covenant topped by the two winged cherubim: one represents God, and the other represents human beings. The Divine voice heard by man emerges from between these two cherubim:

> When Moses arrived at the Tent of Meeting to speak with Him, he heard the voice speaking to him from atop the cover that was upon the Ark of the Testimony, from between the two cherubim, and He spoke to him (Numbers 7:89).

The space in the Holy of Holies above the cherubim belongs to the Divine, while the area beneath is human territory. The place where the human and Divine meet is between the cherubim. The parallel in human beings to this focal point of the Ark in the Holy of Holies, is the portion of the soul known as *ruach*, or spirit and its physical place, the human heart.

One way to understand how God speaks to us in dreams is to understand the anatomy of the soul according to Jewish tradition. The human soul has three parts—*neshama*, *nefesh*, and *ruach*. Each of these soul aspects has a physical counterpart in the human body that serves as an antenna perfectly attuned to receiving and translating spiritual signals into the language of physicality.

At the core of our being we have a *neshama* which is always connected to God, so that it is difficult to tell where the divine presence ends and the person begins. This *neshama* is connected to our *ruach*, our spiritual selves, which is, in turn, is connected to our *nefesh*, our little animal soul, the life force and instinctual energy that burns within us and drives us.

The brain captures and translates the message of the *neshama* into concepts and ideas. The heart collects the signals of the *ruach* and translates them into character, emotions, and speech. The liver is dedicated to the *nefesh* and translates its messages into desires and drives.

The *neshama* is above man's level. The *nefesh*, akin to the life force in ani-mals, is beneath man. The *ruach* perfectly represents man's essential spiritual level. The human heart serves as the physical antenna and receiver of the spiritual force of *ruach* and is the exact counterpart of the place between the cherubim above the Ark in the Holy of Holies.

SHEKHINA, DREAMS, and THE WORLD OF FORMATION

Sleep is one-sixtieth of death . . . .
(Zohar I, 206b-207a)

Therefore, just before falling asleep a person sees the souls of all his dead relatives and all share his soul root. Since sleep is only one sixtieth of death this insight might flash before one's eyes very quickly. A great *tzaddek* will see them very clearly, but others may see or feel only a vague impression.

Rodger Kamenetz in his book *The History of Last Night's Dream* summarizes the recent studies of the brain's neuroanatomy and dreaming: During sleep the parts of the brain that govern lower activity are turned off. When we are asleep the dorsal-lateral prefrontal cortex that is dedicated to the where and what of waking life is disconnected or unlinked. The *precuneus*, which governs brief moment-to-moment memory, autobiographical recall, and spatial ori-entation, is also turned off. The body too sleeps: With the exception of the diaphragm and the eyeball muscles and an occasional twitch, our large mus-cle groups are paralyzed. All these brain and muscle functions, our helpers in daily life, go to sleep. This loss, I believe, is experienced as a small death.

While these parts of the body and brain sleep, the various parts of the limbic system—the amygdala and the hypothalamus, which govern emotions and feelings, and which receive auditory and visual stimulation—are more highly awake. And thus it is that we dream...

When the patriarch Jacob was on his death bed he called his sons to his bedside (Genesis 49:3-7) for instruction and blessing. Jacob made them face their past mistakes, their responsibilities, and their lives in the future. Rashi says that this teaching was a necessary condition for the children of Israel to grow straight and true.

Rabbi Nachman of Breslov taught that each person before he goes to sleep should follow Jacob's example and review his experience of the day, and in this way redress his spiritual wounds, regrets and concerns. Reb Nachman wrote that it is good to speak from your heart to God as you would speak to a good and true friend. This is the root of your soul that you can see every night, and that you will see when your time comes to leave this world. If you do this practice each night before sleep you will receive as Jacob's sons did, these gifts of peace of mind for yourself, wisdom and concern for others. This work with the root of one's soul is a kind of bedtime *shma. It is also a tried and true method of dream induction.*

The lowest Sefira on the Kabbalists' Tree of Life and Death is *Malcuth,* also called the *Shekhina.* The *Shekhina* contains *Din,* or Judgment which also has an element of death. A person should prepare himself for sleep by saying *I entrust my life to God.* In this way he consciously entrusts his soul to the *Shekhina* in its proximity to the tree of Death. Since it is forbidden not to return a pledge to the giver when he demands its return, this conscious giving of one's soul over to the *Shekhina* opens the way for the soul's ascent and its return to the living body upon awakening.

The Zohar describes the soul's night journey more poetically:

So the soul mounts up, returning to its source, whilst the body lies still as a stone, thus reverting to its own source of origin. . . . There are night attendants who have charge of these souls, take them up on high. . . . The supreme chieftain of those regions bears the name *Suriya,* and each soul, as it passes through all the firmaments, is first brought before him, and he inhales its scent... the scent of the fear of the LORD. . . . He takes them under his charge, and passes them on higher. . . . There all the souls are absorbed in the Shekhina, the Supreme Point; as a woman conceives a child, so does the Supreme Point conceive them, experiencing a rapturous pleasure (Zohar II, 213b).

The prayer that frightens many children—*Now I lay me down to sleep. . . . If I should die before I wake, I pray the Lord my soul to take...*—is based on the same principle. Each night a person experiences the small death of sleep. Then, the *neshama*, or part of the soul leaves the body and ascends through the firmaments or three worlds of Sefirot gathering spiritual wisdom, revelations and insights. The Zohar says that each night the angels wait and delay their singing until the souls of the righteous seekers join them. Then they sing together to God on high and *The flowers appear on the earth; the time of the singing of birds is come, and the voice of the turtle is heard in our land* (Song of Songs 2:12). Rabbi Judah adds that this is also what is meant by *Let them sing aloud upon their beds* (Psalms 149:5).

In the Zohar, Rabbi Hiya discourses on the subject of dreams citing this text:

> And he said, Hear now my words: If there be a prophet among you, I the LORD do make myself known unto him in a vision, In a dream I will speak with him (Numbers 12:6).

Rabbi Hiya explains:

> Come and see. The Holy One, blessed be He made many different levels, and they all coexist one upon the other, level upon level, one above the other. . . . Come and see. Every proper dream derives from this level, and these levels are seen through a mirror in which all the colors may be seen, a mirror that does not shine (I, 183a-183b).

The *Shekhina* is the Supreme Point and receives the influences of all the Sefirot, and reflects all their colors. The *Shekhina* is the mirror that does not shine. The Hebrew word for a phenomenal vision, *marah* also means mirror.

Rabbi Hiya continues:

> *"In a dream, in a vision of the night, when deep sleep falls upon men, in slumber upon the bed, He opens the ears of men, and seals their instruction"* (Job 33:15-16). When men lie asleep upon their beds and their souls leave them and soar aloft— the Holy One, blessed be He, informs the soul, through the particular level of the angel Gabriel that is in charge of dreams of things that are to happen in the world, or of things with which the dreamer is preoccupied so that man may receive correc-

tion in the world. A man is not given information while he is enjoying bodily vigour, as we have said, but the angel informs the soul and the soul informs the man, and the dream is there in the world above when the souls leave their bodies and ascend, each one taking its own route. There are many levels in the mystery of Wisdom. Come and see. Dream is one level, and vision is one level, and prophesy is one level, and they are levels one above the other (Zohar I, 183a).

When the soul has ascended, gathered wisdom from the many levels, and sung with the angels, morning nears and the *neshama* descends. It passes by the Tree of Life, and returns to the body where its experiences of the worlds above are formed into dreams.

The Zohar advises:

At night let a man ponder on the fact that he will have departed from the world and his soul will leave him, and the Lord of all will restore it, for every night the Supreme Point, the mystery of the womb of the *Shekhina* receives within it the souls of the righteous.... as a woman conceives a child, so does the Supreme Point conceive them, experiencing a rapturous pleasure in absorbing the souls in itself... The souls then re-emerge, that is to say, they are born anew, each soul being fresh and new as at its original birth (Zohar II, 213b-214a).

The Zohar (II, 213b-214a) explains this supreme mystery saying:

...This is the inner meaning of the words, "*They are new every morning; great is thy faithfulness*" (Lamentations 3:23). That is to say they—the souls—are new every morning because the Shekhina ("*great is thy faithfulness*") is eager to absorb them and then let them out newly born.

The *Shekhina* as the Supreme Point stands ready, faithful to her essential womb nature. Like a woman, she conceives the soul with rapture and pleasure. The *Shekhina* womb needs the goodness of the soul, and the soul needs the acceptance of the *Shekhina*, and the wisdom and meaning given in the dream. The *Shekhina* sends the soul out of the womb renewed and reborn. Again the mutual reciprocal need of God the indwelling *Shekhina* for human beings, and the need of human beings for knowing and experiencing God.

Upon arising one can say the traditional prayer: *Modeh ani lefenecha.....I give thanks before you, living and eternal King for you have returned my soul within me, with compassion. Abundant is Your faithfulness.* Following this declaration one may remember the instruction of the soul's night journey. Even when the mirror is dull and hazy and one does "not remember" meaning comes. Writing one's dreams, or simply writing anything at all about one's state of being upon awakening opens the way.

Rabbi Moshe Chayim Luzzatto, in his classic book *The Way of God*, explains that during sleep, when the body and senses are at rest, and only the imagination is awake, a part of the soul from the side of spirit and above, or *ruach*, called the *neshama*, leaves the body in the care of the lower or animal soul, the *nefesh*. The *neshama* soul goes flying up to all the spiritual realms of heaven seeking to know God. There the freed *neshama* encounters angels and prophesy, and also demons and *sheddim*. In the soul's journey it learns a bit about future events in the world, matters of personal concern to the dreamer, and it is given all manner of wisdom and understanding.

The higher soul, the *neshama* returns and transmits this experience step by step to the animal soul. Thus, the person's imagination is stimulated and forms a dream. Since the dream is formed in the imagination by information coming from both angels and demons and, Luzzatto adds, even from what one has eaten that day and the body's own hormones, the dream may seem too full or obscure, or it may be perfectly clear. A person may even be given information about the future if God so decrees.

Writing the dream fully, including one's immediate thoughts and feelings brings a sense of completion, wholeness, well being and renewal.

Dream Instruction

The Bible is full of dreams, visions of the night that give the dreamer personal instruction from a divine source. The Bible also contains many serious warnings against listening to false prophets who say that their own personal dreams are prophetic visions. These "filthy dreamers" or *enupniazomai* (en-oop-nee-ad'-zom-ahee) as they are called in the Greek versions of the Bible, are beguiled with sensual images and carried away to an impious course of conduct. They are also charlatans who pervert the essentially divine meaning of dreams to their own private power drives. The prophet Jeremiah writes of his despair at these false dreamers and false prophets:

> … the land is full of adulterers; for because of swearing the land mourneth; the pleasant places of the wilderness are dried up, and their course is evil, and their force is not right (Jeremiah 23:10).

And the Lord replies:

> I have heard what the prophets said, that prophesy lies in my name, saying, I have dreamed, I have dreamed. How long shall this be in the heart of the prophets that prophesy lies? Yea, they are prophets of the deceit of their own heart (Jeremiah 23:25-26).

> Therefore, behold, I am against the prophets, saith the LORD, that steal my words every one from his neighbour. Behold, I am against the prophets, saith the LORD, that use their tongues, and say, He saith. Behold, I am against them that prophesy false dreams, saith the LORD, and do tell them…. I sent them not, nor commanded them (Jeremiah 23:30-33).

[When you] . . . call upon me, and ye shall go and pray unto me, and I will hearken unto you. And ye shall seek me, and find me, when ye shall search for me with all your heart. And I will be found of you, saith the LORD (Jeremiah 29:12-15).

When a person begins to do this soulful form of dreamwork he or she calls upon God, and seeks to know God with all his heart, God will hear his prayers and each person will be responsible for himself. God will make a new individual covenant with each of his people:

Behold, the days come, saith the LORD, that I will make a new covenant with the people.... Not according to the covenant that I made with their fathers . . . . But this shall be the covenant ... saith the LORD, I will put my law in their inward parts, and write it in their hearts; and will be their God, and they shall be my people (Jeremiah 31:29-33).

It is said that the name of the law, *Torah*, is *moreh*, teacher. The new covenant is that God will put his divine instruction—*meaning*—into a person's inward parts, and write it in a person's heart. This new covenant means that meaning, divine instruction, is given as personal correction and direction. Teaching is given to each individual personally.

The Hebrew word *kereb* that is translated as "inward part" means a physical sense that is the both the seat and the faculty of thought and emotion. A secondary, but important meaning is "entrails," as in the entrails of sacrificial animals. The Hebrew lexicon defines the word as meaning "come near," "approach," and even approach a woman sexually. There is no mistake in meaning. The new covenant of individual responsibility for those who want to know the Self will result in God coming close to them, putting *meaning*, divine correction and instruction, into each person's inner parts, and writing it on each person's heart. In this way each person will know Self intimately from his or her own inner experience and each in his or her own heart.

This promise of divine instruction known and felt in one's inner parts, and in one's heart, will come to anyone who calls to God, or prays, or seeks God with all his or her heart. The Bible is full of personal dreams that are described and interpreted. Dreams are longed for in times of personal crisis. Dreams instruct, inspire, predict, and heal, but they are never intended as teachings for all. The true miracle of the dream lies in its personal and individual meaningfulness. The Book of Job assures us:

> God speaketh once, yea twice, yet man perceiveth it not. In a dream, in a vision of the night, when deep sleep falleth upon men, in slumberings upon the bed; Then he openeth the ears of men, and sealeth their instruction (Job 33:14-16).

"And Joseph dreamed a dream . . ." (Genesis 35:6) begins Rabbi Hiya's discourse on dreams in the Zohar. And then he goes on to say:

> The dream is a sixtieth part of prophesy . . . which is the grade of Gabriel supervisor of dreams . . . the word has power over it, and . . . every dream needs a good interpretation (Zohar II 183a).

The word has power over the dream and determines how the dream will be experienced by the dreamer, and what it will mean to him or her. Although the dream originates in the realm of Gabriel, the real meaning of the dream is expressed in words by the *Shekhina*, the divine presence that rules speech.

Rabbi Hiya cites the Bible story of Joseph who understood the *true* meaning of the butler's and the baker's dreams. The chief butler of Pharaoh tells his experience to Pharaoh:

> Pharaoh was wroth with his servants, and put me in the captain of the guard's house, *both* me and the chief baker: And we dreamed a dream in one night, I and he; we dreamed each man according to the interpretation of his dream. And *there was* there with us a young man, an Hebrew, servant to the captain of the guard; and we told him, and he interpreted to us our dreams; to each man according to his dream he did interpret. And it came to pass, as he interpreted to us, so it was; me he restored unto mine office, and him he hanged (Genesis 41:9-14).

Pharaoh then sent for Joseph, the young Hebrew man who had truly understood and interpreted the dreams of his butler and the baker, and told the meaning of each man's dream, and Pharaoh said:

> I have dreamed a dream, and *there is* none that can interpret it: and I have heard say of thee, *that* thou canst understand a dream to interpret it. And Joseph answered Pharaoh, saying, *It is* not in me: God shall give Pharaoh an answer of peace (Genesis 41:15-16).

This is a terribly important point. I do not interpret my patient's dreams. The true meaning of a dream comes from the dreamer. It is a gift form God. I teach people to listen to their dreams, to hear the divine instruction. I do this by listening and hearing their dreams and my own. After this book had been written and was still in manuscript state, I gave it to a friend to read. He in turn gave it to his friend, Rodger Kamenetz, who had just published his dream book. Rodger and I met and we too became friends. We discovered that we both had children who had gone to Yale and had been, synchronistically, in the same college. Rodger too had been at Yale, at that college. Rodger and I read each other's books.

Both Rodger and I were writing "Jewish" dream books but we come to dreamwork from totally opposite directions. I dreamt:

> *I am in a building complex. [Jung used the term complex to mean an emotionally charged psychic entity]. It is It is Yale University. It is high on a hill, Each time I go outside, from any part of the building I see that the hillside is very steep, almost concave and covered with ice. It is like the depression I can fly over by the seat of my pants in the earlier dream of my childhood home. This time when I am seventy, I must stay in the warm sunny Yale until the frozen hillside melts.*

Why Yale? I asked in the active imagination. Immediately I knew that it was because I had not gone there as an undergraduate, and now I had to spend time there. I had whizzed through college in three years. Now I needed to tarry as Moses did in the story of the burning bush. The soul is slow and needs time.

Then, in time, I remembered that the seal of Yale University had Hebrew letters on it. What do they mean? I learned from Google, not active imagination, that the letters spell Urim v'Tumim, the oracle worn by the High Priest of the ancient Temple in Jerusalem. These words are traditionally translated by Yale scholars to mean Light and Truth, or sometimes Light and Perfection. These words are not usually translated at all by Jewish scholars. I had not translated them when I wrote about them in my book about Amulets and Talismans.

I understood that the dream was instructing me to take the time to translate my wildly intuitive mystical dream book into a more understandable language, and to use time and words to make it more understandable and meaningful to people. I want this book and the process of soulful dreamwork to bring Light and Truth and even enlightenment and Perfection or wholeness.

As the Zohar says, every dream comes from a lower level and speech is superior to that grade. Thus, the word has power over the dream. The *Shekhina* has power over speech, and is superior to the angel Gabriel, the prince of dreams. The divine instruction of the dream is expressed and revealed through the *Shekhina* the indwelling divine presence. As Joseph says, it is not his interpretation, but, God's that makes the dream "come true." It is in that sense of having a true personal meaning for the dreamer, or what Rabbi Hiya calls "a good interpretation" that a dream is one sixtieth prophesy.

Pharaoh tells Joseph his dream:

And Pharaoh said unto Joseph, In my dream, behold, I stood upon the bank of the river: And, behold, there came up out of the river seven kine, fat fleshed and well favoured; and they fed in a meadow: And, behold, seven other kine came up after them, poor and very ill favoured and lean fleshed, such as I never saw in all the land of Egypt for badness: And the lean and the ill favoured kine did eat up the first seven fat kine: And when they had eaten them up, it could not be known that they had eaten them; but they *were* still ill favoured, as at the beginning. So I awoke.

Apparently as often happens, Pharaoh dreamt, awoke, and then dreamt again,

> …. And I saw in my dream, and, behold, seven ears came up in one stalk, full and good: And, behold, seven ears, withered, thin, *and* blasted with the east wind, sprung up after them: And the thin ears devoured the seven good ears: and I told *this* unto the magicians; but *there was* none that could declare *it* to me (Genesis 41:17-25).

Joseph says to Pharaoh, "The dream of Pharaoh *is* one: God has shown Pharaoh exactly what he *is* about to do." Both dreams are one says Joseph because they have the same meaning. Moreover, the dream itself is one with its meaning. Each word is just as it says. Joseph repeats:

> The seven good kine *are* seven years; and the seven good ears *are* seven years: *the dream is one*. And the seven thin and ill favoured kine that came up after them *are* seven years; and the seven empty ears blasted with the east wind shall be seven years of famine. This *is* the thing which I have spoken unto Pharaoh: What God *is* about to do he sheweth unto Pharaoh (Genesis 41:26-29).

And Joseph adds for good measure:

> And for that the dream was doubled unto Pharaoh twice; *it is* because the thing *is* established by God, and God will shortly bring it to pass (Genesis 41:32).

The Zohar uses these passages from the Bible to show that dreams come from God, and have meaning. As a Jungian analyst I know that a true understanding of a dream, a "good interpretation" as Rabbi Hiya says, does have a profound influence on what happens, and what comes to pass. It often happens that a dream is doubled, or repeated until its full meaning is understood. Each person has his own mythology and dream world. In addition to the archetypal universal symbols and images, certain images and situations become a standard personal vocabulary for a dreamer. These images change and develop in future dreams as the dreamer takes the meaning to heart.

The rabbis in the Zohar continue talking about this mystery: How does dream interpretation and understanding influence a dream? How is a dream divine instruction, or even divine correction? Is a "true interpretation" the same as the dream's meaning?

The Old Testament tells this story: Joseph's father Jacob loved Joseph more than all his children, because he was the son of his old age. He made Joseph a coat of many colors. Joseph then dreamed a dream, and he told it to his brothers:

> We *were* binding sheaves in the field, and, lo, my sheaf arose, and also stood upright; and, behold, your sheaves stood round about, and made obeisance to my sheaf. And his brethren said to him, Shalt thou indeed reign over us? or shalt thou indeed have dominion over us? And they hated him yet the more for his dreams, and for his words (Genesis 37:2-5).

This dream too is doubled like Pharaoh's dream:

> And he dreamed yet another dream, and told it his brethren, and said, Behold, I have dreamed a dream more; and, behold, the sun and the moon and the eleven stars made obeisance to me. And he told *it* to his father, and to his brethren: and his father rebuked him, and said unto him, What *is* this dream that thou hast dreamed? Shall I and thy mother and thy brethren indeed come to bow down ourselves to thee to the earth? And his brethren envied him; but his father observed the saying (Genesis 37:5-12).

The Rabbis in the Zohar discuss the fact that Joseph told his dreams to his brothers. The dreams predict, correctly, that Joseph will rule over his brothers and his parents. The rabbis claim that the "interpretation" came true. They say that because the dreams, or Joseph's telling his dreams to his brothers, made his brothers hate him, the dream's meaningful intention was delayed for twenty-two years. I believe that this is an example of how a person can either choose to seek divine instruction with an open heart, and try to understand the true meaning of his soul's night time journeys, or he can use and misuse the dream to his own detriment.

The Zohar continues:

> Rabbi Hiya and Rabbi Jose used to study with Rabbi Simeon. Rabbi Hiya once put to him the following question: 'We have learned that an uninterpreted dream is like an unopened letter (Talmud Berekhot 55a). Does this mean that the dream comes true, but without the dreamer being conscious of it, or that it will not be fulfilled at all?'

Rabbi Simeon replied:

> The dream comes true, but without the dreamer being aware of it. For nothing happens in the world that has not been announced in the world by what is made known in advance either by means of a dream or a proclamation.

> Rabbi Simeon explained ... in the time of the prophets God promised to make his intentions known to his servants, the prophets (Amos 3:7),... When prophets were no more, their place was taken by sages. . . . In the absence of Sages, things to come are revealed in dreams, and if not in dreams, the matter may be found in the of the birds in the sky (Zohar II, 183a).

Joseph paid no attention to the true personal instructional and correctional meaning of the dream. Instead, he pridefully told his dreams to his brothers, and caused them to hate him even more than they did already. They then threw him into a pit and intended to kill him. The caravan of slave trader came along, and the brothers decided to sell Joseph to the slave trader, who then sold Joseph into slavery in Egypt. Eventually, when there was famine in their own land, the brothers and their father Jacob were forced to beg for food from Joseph who had by then risen to a place of authority in Pharaoh's realm. A "good interpretation," or a true personal understanding of the meaning of the dream by Joseph, would have resulted in a different and more immediate outcome.

Later, when Jacob is dying, the entire matter rises to the surface again. The brothers are said to believe that Joseph will indeed take revenge upon them for their having thrown him into the pit. Indeed, Joseph had recognized his brothers immediately upon their arrival in Egypt, but did not tell them that. Instead, he puts them through an emotional roller coaster. He sends them back to get their father and his youngest brother, Benjamin. Some *midrashim* say that Joseph does this *so that* his dream may come true, and all will bow down to him. Psychologically, Joseph acts out against his father and brothers precisely because he hasn't taken the dream personally as divine instruction.

Words and instruction mean that the elements in the dream are parts of one's own psyche, projected upon others; in this case the brothers and the parents. Joseph is now in the service of Pharaoh and acts out of a power driven for revenge instead of achieving psychological and spiritual integration. It is no wonder that Jacob makes Joseph swear that he will bring his bones back to Canaan. Jacob does not want his grave in Egypt to become a shrine for idol worship. The difference is between an inward God who gives personal divine instruction and correction, and a Pharaonic idol worshipping God, where Pharaoh is God, and all powerful is anathema to Jacob, and true, meaningful, soulful dreamwork.

The Word Has Power Over the Dream

Hebrew is a modular language. All the words have a three, or rarely, a four letter root, or shoresh, which can be modified by a vowel or letter change into an entire family of connotative meaning. Thus the root *shin, mem, aleph,* which makes the word *sh'ma,* or "hear," can also mean "listen," "understand," "inform," and "report." The image of a rose is closest to what I am describing. The essence is in each petal, while the petals themselves differ from each other in several ways. Each petal may have a different hue, or shape, or position, or intensity of scent, but all are essentially rose.

Meaning in dreams is conveyed in the same way. There is an essence of meaning, and the structure, sequence, images, language, mood, and atmosphere of the dream all contrive to express that meaning in its complexity and in its entirety. The dream has a connotative as well as a denotative meaning. True understanding of a dream moves one toward integration and wholeness, not merely toward linear, reductive analysis, and fact. Abulafia writes,

> You feel an extra spirit awakening within yourself and strengthening you and passing over your entire body and giving you pleasure, and it will seem to you that fine balm has been poured over you from the crown of your head to your feet, once or many times. You shall rejoice and feel from it a great pleasure, with gladness and trembling (Abulafia, *Qzar 'Eden Ganuz*).

The trembling, Abulafia writes, comes from the struggle between the Active Intellect and the Imagination. Psychologically, this is the fear and awe human beings have of God, and the relationship between the ego and the Self.

THE LIGHTS IN THE LETTERS

The word has interpretive power over the dream, and the word has an essential root of meaning. The word is made of letters, and each letter has an essence of its own. Dov Baer, the Maggid of Medzedek, said:

> The lights in the letters are God's chambers, into which he transmits his emanations. Place all your thoughts into the power of your words until you see the light of the words. You can then see how one word shines into another, and how many lights are brought forth in their midst (Aryeh Kaplan, in *Chassidic Masters*, 40).

The linguist and rabbi Joel Hoffman (author of *In The Beginning: The Origins of the Hebrew Language*) writes brilliantly about the origins of the Hebrew language. The letters used in the Hebrew alphabet are essentially the same as those used by the Phoenicians and others in the Ancient world and have become the Roman letters used today in English and many other alphabets. However, all the letters of the Phoenician and early Hebrew alphabet were consonants. Only the scribes and learned people could read or write and understand the meaning of a word. That is the letters *bet tav* (ב ת) could be *biet* (house) or *bat* (daughter). In order for many people to read and write, and understand writing, and derive meaning from it, the Hebrews had to invent vowels. The first Hebrew vowels were the letters which were originally used as consonants: *yud, heh,* and *vav.* These, not surprisingly, are the very letters that comprise the tetragammatron, or magic, ineffable name of God, *yud, heh, vav, heh.*

For Jewish mystics, the Hebrew letters assume great importance. The letters are divine lights or energy patterns. The Sefer Yetzirah explains that the World of Emanation was created

> in thirty-two mysterious paths of Wisdom, *Yah* Eternal of Hosts *Yud-Vav-Yud,* God of Israel, Living *Elohim,* Almighty God, High and Extolled, Dwelling in Eternity, Holy Be His Name, engraved and created His world in three *Sefirim:* in writing, number and word. Ten *Sefirot* out of nothing, twenty-two foundation letters (Chapter One of Sefer Yetzirah).

After creating the World of Emanation with an outpouring of the letters (sparks), God paired each letter with every other letter and created *she'arim*, or gates, to all possible meanings. The Sefer Yetzirah continues:

> Twenty-two letters: He carved them, hewed them, refined them, weighed them, and combined them, and He made of them the entire creation and everything to be created in the future. How did He test them? *Alef* with all and all with *Alef, Bet* with all and all with *Bet, Gimel* with all and all with *Gimel,* and they all return again and again, and they emanate through two hundred and thirty-one gates. All the words and all the creatures emanate from One Name (Chapter Four of Sefer Yetzirah).

The Saadia Gaon adds his commentary to the original story in the Sefer Yetzirah of the twenty-two letters of creation:

> When we say that it is by means of these media that the Eternal, Master of hosts, God of Israel, Living Elohim, Almighty, Sufficient, Noble and Sublime, Dwelling in Eternity, Holy Be His Name has traced the twenty-two letters according to the construction of the sphere, we refer to the sphere's rotation which displaces to the rear what was positioned to the fore. It is the same with the letters when one inverts them, putting to the rear what had been at the fore. Proof of this is demonstrated when one says *oneg*, delight which is something desirable, and when one says *nega*, plague which is something detestable: the letters are the same, only inverted.
>
> This verse is the pivotal point of the book, namely that the Creator —Holy Be His Name—has so disposed some of the letters and numbers to create a kind of body. Later He transposed their positions in order to create a body different from the first.

Dreams happen and are experienced visually and emotionally, and sometimes merely conceptually. They can be given body or told with words, and words must be made with letters. The Hebrew alphabet is called the letters of creation. The word for letter is *ot*. It means a sign and a wonder, and has the connotative meaning of creation. The process of creation described in the book of Genesis from the first letter, *bet*, of Bereshit, to the first *bet* of *tohu v'bohu*—without form and void—contains the 42 letter name of God. It can be interpreted as an endless stream of letters poured forth from heaven to earth. Thought of in this way, the letters bring a thing into being. If there is no written or verbal designation for a thing, it is no thing. Schneur Salman of Ladi, the first Lubuvitcher Rebbe known as the alte Rebbe, writes about the letters of creation in his brilliant exposition on creation, *Tanya:* Volume III pp. 838-839. He writes,

> God said: Let there be a firmament between the waters (Genesis I:6). These words and letters through which the heavens were created stand firmly forever within the firmament of heaven. Similarly, every thing created by God must constantly and ceaselessly be vested with the divine life force which created it. If the creative letters were to depart even for an instant and return to their source—God—all the heavens would become naught and absolutely nothingness, and it would be as though they had never existed at all, exactly as before the utterance, *Let there be a firmament . . .*

> Even within that which appears to be utterly inanimate matter, such as stones or earth or water, there is a soul and spiritual life force. Although they evince no demonstrable form of animation, within them are nevertheless, the letters of speech from the ten utterances of creation in the Book of Genesis which give life and existence to inanimate matter, enabling it to come into being out of the naught and nothingness that preceded the six days of creation.

The Alte Rebbe continues:

> The name *evan* or stone is not mentioned in the ten utterances. How can we then say that the letters of the ten utterances are enclothed within a stone? (*Tanya*, 840-841).

He goes on to explain, as the Sefer Yetzirah does, that the twenty-two letters of the Hebrew alphabet in two letter combinations form 462 pairs. Half of these are exact reversals of each other, i.e., *aleph-bet* and *bet-aleph*. The 231 remaining pairs are the gates to meaning. The names of all creatures in the holy tongue are the very letters of speech which descend degree by degree, from the ten utterances recorded in the first ten sentences of the Torah. By a process of substitution and transposition the letters pass through the 231 gates until they reach a particular created thing and become invested in it, thereby giving it life.

Because the letters themselves are holy, meditation on even one letter of the Hebrew alphabet results in meaningful experience. The Ari taught that the first letter of the Hebrew alphabet, *aleph*, speaks of the paradox of God and man. He wrote that because the *aleph* is formed by two *yuds* (ר) one to the upper right and the other to the lower left, joined by a diagonal *vav* (ו).

Aleph

These represent the higher and lower waters and the firmament between them. Water is first mentioned in the Torah in the account of the first day of Creation, *And the spirit of God hovered over the surface of the water* (Genesis 1:2). At this time the higher and the lower waters were indistinguishable; their state is referred to as water in water. On the second day of creation God separated the two waters by stretching the firmament between them.

In the service of the soul, as taught in *Chassidut*, the higher water is water of joy, the experience of being close to God, while the lower water is water of bitterness, the experience of being far from God.

The Talmud tells of four sages who entered the "Pardes," the mystical orchard of the deepest spiritual knowing. The greatest of the four, Rabbi Akiva, said to the others before entering, "When you come to the place of pure marble stone, do not say 'water-water'. The Ari explains that the place of pure marble stone is where the higher and the lower waters unite. Here one must not call out 'water-water,' as if to divide the higher and lower waters." The place of pure marble stone is the place of truth—the Divine power to bear two opposites simultaneously. Rabbi Shalom ben Adret calls this the paradox of paradoxes because here the exaltation of God and His closeness to man unite with the lowliness of man and his distance from God.

A woman had been practicing meditation and calligraphy with the Hebrew letters for years. She always carried with her two very different but equally precious to her, italic pens. She practiced writing all the letters of the alphabet until she had learned it and from then on she practiced only *alephs*. She drew them, and tried to make them as she saw them on scrolls, She tried different styles. When she first came upon this teaching of the Ari she could not see the two *yuds* in the *aleph* at all; not when she looked at it and not when she drew it. Then, she lost the more "male" of the two pens.

A few days later she dreamt of dancing, flaming *alephs*. When she drew the *alephs* of the dream, she saw the two *yuds*.. If you turn the *aleph* upside down, reversing the upper and lower waters, the *aleph* looks just the same. Above and below are mirror images of each other. And between the two *yuds*, is a *vav*. It is actually a reversed *vav* or a double *vav*. The reversed *vav* is the place where the higher and lower waters unite. It is the place where God and man are closest. The union of higher reality, the upper *yud*, with the lower reality, the lower *yud*, by means of the connecting *vav* of *Torah*, is the ultimate secret of the letter *aleph*.

Just as the *aleph* has the unique ability to reverse itself, so has the letter *vav* a unique and profoundly meaningful grammatical power in Biblical Hebrew. Adding a *vav*, ‫ו‬, a single stroke of a letter to the beginning of a verb means "and." It transforms the past perfect and completed happening to the future imperfect, intended, conditional, and continuing happening. Thus, "was," with the wonderful transformative wand of a *vav*, becomes "was," "will be," "shall be," and "is." Conversely, adding this stroke of *vav* to the beginning of an imperfect verb changes it from an intended future action to one that has already happened, and is continuing to happen. The Bible tells the story of what has happened, is happening, and will continue to happen.

Each Hebrew letter is holy and meaningful and may be used as a device for meditation and spiritual development. Each letter has a numerical equivalent: *aleph* is one, *bet* is two, and so on. Words with a similar numerical value may share a hidden meaningful connection. This sort of letter and number substitution is called *gematria*.

In another practice of Jewish mystics called *notarikon*, words are broken down into sentences composed of initial letters. Thus, the first word of the Ten Commandments, *anokhi*, "I Am," can mean the sentence *Ario Nafshoy Katovit Yahovit* —"I have written and given myself to you in this book."

All Israel is said to have seen the letters come flying forth at Mount Sinai from North and East and South, and every direction. Because of the encoded significance of the word *anokhi* we believe God gave Moses not just the Ten Commandments at Sinai, but the entire *Torah*. The letters of *Torah* were white fire engraved with black fire (*Shir ha-Shirim Rabbah 1:13*).

> Now they came forth, these carved flaming letters flashing like gold when it dazzles. Like a craftsman smelting silver and gold: when he takes them out of the blazing fire all is bright and pure; so the letters came forth pure and bright from the flowing measure of the spark.
>
> Therefore it is written: , *"The word of YHVH is refined"* (*Psalms 18:31*), as silver and gold are refined. When these letters came forth , they were all refined, carved precisely, sparkling, flashing. All of Israel saw the letters flying thru space in every direction, engraving themselves on the tablet of stone (*Zohar, The Book of Enlightenment*, Daniel Chanan Matt, trans., 119-120).

At creation with the outpouring of the ten utterances, and again at Mount Sinai, God manifests as letters. The flaming engraved letters, "*and the tablets were the work of God, and the writing was the writing of God, graven upon the tablets*" (Exodus 32:16).

Nachmanides taught that a Torah scroll is written with no vowel points because there should not be only one way to read Torah. A Sefer Torah is not pointed because it contains all the ways and methods of interpretation, both inner and outer, and they may all be interpreted through each and every letter, aspects within aspects, secrets within secrets, and it has no limit known to us. From the edge of every letter in the Torah heaps upon heaps of interpretation are suspended.

One needs to let the letters dance. Abulafia, who practiced an ecstatic form of Kabbalah, suggests a form of meditation where a person permutates all the possible letter combinations of a word. For example: using the word heart. One finds: heat, eat, ate, rate, hate, ear, hear, tear (from an eye), tear (a piece of paper), tea, are, art, hart, at, hat, rat, tar, he, her, the, that, earth.

> There is no word in the torah that does not contain many secrets, many reasons, many roots, many branches (Zohar II, 55b).

The Zohar continues,

> We have learned that as soon as a new interpretation of Torah leaves a man's mouth it ascends and is presented to the Holy One, blessed be He, and the Holy one, blessed be he receives it , and kisses it, and adorns it with seventy engraved crowns...Then the Ancient of Days savors the scent of this new interpretation and gains great satisfaction from it (Zohar I, 73b, III, 83b, 118a).

Much of what these Jewish mystics have written and believed and practiced in their Torah study is equally true in soulful dreamwork. The essential meaning of a dream is in the words of the dream. These are the words used to describe, create, and make meaningful the images and the experience of the dream.

One of the well known, often repeated Kabbalistic instructions for meditating on God's name begins: sit in a room, alone, with a pen and ink and a tablet. This is equally true for soulful dreamwork. The intention must be present for understanding a dream. The dreamer must welcome the dream and remember it. Writing the dream helps. As you write, more is remembered, with meaning already emerging. These ideas too should be included in the written dream. The essence of meaning is what the Zohar means by "a good interpretation." Practice *hitbedout,* wrapped in a condition of aloneness: Meditate on a dream, alone, without knowing, and with an open heart. Breathe deeply and regularly and naturally. When the breathing is natural, the body, and the ego have surrendered and opened to another universe of meaning. This is a beginning and an opening. Think of the lovely Hebrew word *ruach*—spirit ...

This word *ruach* is used in the Hebrew Bible to mean breath, wind, spirit, life, mind, animation, vivacity, vigour, courage, agitation, anger, patience and impatience. It means disposition as troubled, bitter, discontented, and it also means prophetic spirit, and gift. It is the seat of emotion, desire, the spirit of life, and unaccountable and uncontrollable impulses. So when one breathes naturally, one inhales simply what one feels, whatever one feels, and one exhales what one needs: relief, comfort, peace. One begins to know oneself, or one's Self, and the meaning of the dream.

A woman had a very small black lab puppy named Yasmin. A friend gave her a book about dog training written by the well known British dog training expert, Barbara Woodhouse. Ms. Woodhouse began the book by saying that Dog and God were the same word reversed because the dog must think that you are God in order for you to be able to train it. The woman threw the book out.

Years before she had dreamt of a silver and black haired dog running toward her, and coming from afar. She felt that the silver and black dog was a lunar form of the Shekhina, or the moon when she was one of the two Great Lights, before she was diminished, and before the *Shekhina* was sent into exile.

A man dreamt of his beloved's very gentle and loving black dog as one whose sharp teeth were like the thorns around the roses in the Song of Songs (2:3): *"As a rose among thorns so is my darling among the daughters."*

The woman who had dreamt of the silver and black haired dog, years later dreamt of a dog who ran off, leaving her bereft. It went far away but not out of sight, and then to her enormous relief, and joy, it made a grand circle and returned. Dog gone, returned as God, she said, and felt enormous joy.

This woman was reading some of the Kabbalists, who can be very detailed and conceptually overburdened, laying one system upon another. She said,

> I dreamt of a dog so covered and burdened by many layers of shocking pink Indian silk garments, heavily embossed with gold sequins and embroidery, and weighted with rich gold ornaments that I could not tell what kind of dog was under all the coverings, or if indeed, there was a dog under all that stuff. I asked, "Is that my standard poodle?" and was answered in the dream, "Yes."

The sages warn: Woe to anyone who sees only the garments of the Torah, either just the stories or the commandments, and does not see the soul and the root, the real meaning. The woman was looking only at the garments, the conceptual notions of Kabbalah, and they seemed overdone, foreign, and cheap. She was feeling sad and overwhelmed by the Kabbalistic way, and out of touch with herself and her own way of knowing. She asked if that was her dog under all that burden, and was told, "Yes,"—the soul of the Torah, dog/God is there.

The story is the outer garment of the dream. These garments are necessary for the ideas to enter and exist in the psyche. Angels too, like the three who visited Abraham, must don the garments of human beings so that Abraham could see them and hear the message they brought him. The meaning or the message of the dream stories extends to celestial matters and penetrates deeply into supernal mysteries. Under the garments of the dream stories are the mysteries, the soul, and the foundation that is God and called "the soul of souls."

How can one see through to the inner meaning and the divine gift of instruction and correction given in our dreams? The Zohar offers this metaphor:

It is like a girl, beautiful and gracious and much loved, and she is kept closely confined in her palace. She has a special lover, unrecognized by anyone, and concealed. This lover, because of the love that he feels for her, passes by the door of her house , and looks on every side, and she knows that her lover is constantly walking to and fro by the door of her house. What does she do? She opens a tiny door in the secret palace where she lives, and shows her face to her love. Then she withdraws at once and is gone. None of those in her lovers vicinity sees or understands, but her lover alone knows, and his heart and soul and inner being yearn for her, and he knows that it is because of the love that she bears for him that she showed herself to him for a moment, in order to awaken love in him. So it is with the Torah; she reveals herself only to her lover (Isaiah Tishby, *The Wisdom of the Zohar: An Anthology of Texts*, p. 1084).

And so it is with dreams. The Kabbalists speak of the *peshat* level of understanding. This is the simple literal dream or story, and in our metaphor, the beautiful, much loved girl. The second level of interpretation is *remez*, it is more speculative, homiletical and allegorical. The girl opens the door and shows her face to her suitor. She offers a sign and a hint of her true meaning. These are the meanings that become evident even as one writes, remembers, or tells the dream. If the seeker is ready, he takes the next step. He comes closer, and enters the realm of *derash*, or search. He begins to speak to the girl through the veil or curtain that still hides her. Now the two talk with each other, and a deeper exchange and knowing begins. This form of soulful dreamwork is called active imagination. The dreamer dreams the dream on, and actively searches for understanding. The dreamer asks the people or parts of the dream to begin to explain themselves. When he, the seeker, and she, the beloved dream, feel comfortable with each other, she reveals herself to him face to face, and speaks to him of all the mysteries that have lain hidden in her heart. This is the fourth level of understanding, *sod*. The first letter of each of these levels of understanding form PRDS, the mnemonic Pardes, or the orchard of profound mystical knowledge and understanding.

Rabbi Pinchas HaLevi of Barcelona, a well known medieval thinker and teacher wrote the *Sefer HaChinuch*, which is about the 613 Commandments. He wrote that even when God performs major miracles to benefit human beings, He always works them in a hidden way, and they seem to happen in natural ways or in ways close to the natural order. Miracles can only be seen if they can be absorbed through the five ordinary senses.

Rabbi HaLevi teaches that the heavenly fire described in the Talmud (Yuma 21b) took the shape of a lion lying on the altar during the first Temple era, while in the second Temple era it assumed the shape of a reclining dog. The commandment to keep our own earthly fire lit, was intended to render this holy fire visible to the human observer by packaging it in a wrapping that is detectable to our senses.

There is an old form of Hebrew Italian wedding ring that has a gold band surmounted with a tiny square temple. There are towers at the four cor-

ners of the incised stone temple, and a tower at the point where the four triangular roofs of the temple meet. The Hebrew letter *chai*, meaning "life," with a dove on either side of it is positioned as a ladder of ascent to the temple at the top. The temple itself is hinged to the wide band and opens to reveal at the secret heart of the marriage ring, a little square blue enameled plate with the word *Shaddai* on it. This is the magical name for God that is usually translated as God almighty. The Hebrew word *dai* means enough, and *Shaddai* as God almighty encompasses that meaning. At Passover we sing the song of joy and gratitude for our freedom from slavery in Egypt, called *Dayenu*. We praise God, singing

Had God brought us out from Egypt
And not visited them with judgment
It would have been Enough, Dayenu.
Had God visited them with judgment

And not cast down their idols,
Dayenu, it would have been enough.

The song goes on listing the many miracles, and eventually says,

Had God brought us to the foot of Sinai,
And not taught us the Torah—Dayenu.
Had God taught us the Torah
And not brought us into Israel
Dayenu, it would have been enough.

A new understanding of *dai,* "it would have been enough," as part of *Shaddai,* this magical name for God, came as I was writing about the divine gift of dreams, and the deep sense of gratitude, and freedom that understanding dreams gives. One sees the "soul of souls"—God in dreams. One feels grateful not only for the meaning found in soulful dreamwork, but also for the freedom to search and reach, find and create original, real, and personally relevant meaning. This is a true gift. As the triumphal Pesach song of liberation, *Dayenu* says: You gave us Torah, teaching, and that is enough. One can sit alone in a room, at midnight with a pen and a paper in hand. Breathe and allow the second soul to enter your thoughts. Write, reflect, and you receive meaning, revelation and ecstasy. You feel rapture at God's embrace and love comes your way and fills you.

~~

The woman who had been practicing Hebrew calligraphy wrote:

I dreamt of the tiny letter Yud flying from the dense black behind and beyond and coming toward me. It was a gleaming rich yellow gold, and almost immediately after I saw and understood the Yud, a Heh flew toward me, and then a Vav followed closely by another Heh. The letters of the tetragammatron, the magic ineffable name of God. All seemed to originate in the tenth letter, the tiny sperm like Yud.

י

THE FINAL TZADDE

The woman wrote:

> *It was hard to fall asleep on Election Night 2004. So I bathed, and relaxed, turned out the lights, opened the windows and the blinds and watched the wind and lights on the golden trees and dreamt:*
>
> *I heard the distant beep of my little alarm clock. The sun through the shining clean glass was brilliant, then I saw it was eight o'clock, not nine when I usually awaken. Then as I turned toward the light, I saw that beautiful tzadde sofits, final tzaddes drifted down from above. They were red and yellow, dully mirrored with color and arranged in a pattern that showed their balance, grace and depth.*
>
> *I thought, Tzaddek means wise one, or one of the thirty six hidden Lamed Vavs, or Righteous Ones. But Tzaddek begins with the letter tzadde, it does not end with a final tzadde. Later I thought, this is the final tzadde: Those are the colors, red and yellow, love and fear, the human need and desire for meaning and God's love.*
>
> *I had seen the aleph as a flaming dancing letter, with two yuds and a reversing vav. Then I saw the yud as promise, potential, spermatic insemination coming toward me. Yud first, and then yud heh vav heh, the Tetragammatron, the ineffable name for God. The dream of the dull mirror of red and yellow, tzadde sofits of love, need, desire and fear became one "e" to final tzadde, a single open prayerful one.*

Then this woman dreamt:

> *I had sent out six or seven messages carried by tiny angels shaped like Yuds. I was checking, waiting, and hoping... Malachim, the Hebrew word for angels is often translated as "messenger." What these prayers or hopes are I am not sure. I also think that it was six, a half dozen, and a goodly number!*

בּ

In meditating on the letter *bet* בּ this woman had felt its strong solid base, walls, and door to be *biet*, or house. The next night she dreamt,

Something had happened at the place that I was at—that was made secret, or hidden by the empty house across the way. Something had happened in me, the house of me: Bet, biet, it was made secret, hidden by the empty house across the way. I looked over there and decided to investigate. The way between the two houses was flat. The evening darkness lit by and covered with snow.

I set out walking in the ankle deep snow and noticed that it wasn't cold or wet. I didn't feel it. . . I did not continue. Something happened over there at that empty house, and there is a lot of frozen feeling between me and it. Time will tell. I am not ready to traverse that field now, but later when I read about Jacob's dream at Bethel, biet-El, the house of God, and the gate of heaven as he called it I began to feel and understand the meaning of my dream.

Dreams in the Bible

The Bible uses many words to mean dream. There is *chazaw*, an Aramaic word meaning to "see," "behold," or "witness," and also to behold in a dream or vision.

Certainly the word "behold" carries the numinousity of the experience. The Hebrew word used most often is *chalom*. It means to dream ordinary dreams, to dream prophetic dreams, and it is also the word for the dreams of false prophets. The same word also means to be healthy, to be strong, and to restore to health. The very personal dreams of Abimelech, Jacob, Laban, Joseph, of Pharaoh and his servants, the baker and the cupbearer, Balaam, and the more prophetic dream about the demise of the Midianites, and the dreams old men in latter days, and the dreams of false prophets are all described in the Old Testament using the same Hebrew word, *chalom*, to mean dream. The dream of Solomon as a young man, and the dreams Saul longed for when he was smitten with terror of the Philistines, and nightmares of Job, and the dreams understood and interpreted, and the great dream dreamt by Daniel are all called *chalom* in the Hebrew Bible.

In the Old Testament when God has completed the detailed instructions for building the Temple, he begins to describe the garments the High Priest must wear as he performs the sacred Temple rituals. Over finely made linen garments the High Priest wears the breast piece of judgment (the *ephod*) which is a square gold breastplate consisting of four rows of precious gemstones, with three jewels in each row. The third stone in the third row is the *achlomah*, translated as amethyst, and containing the same Hebrew root as the word for dream, *chalom*. Therefore, the achlomah is sometimes called a dream stone.

And Aaron shall bear the names of the children of Israel in the breastplate of judgment upon his heart, when he goeth in unto the holy place, for a remembrance before the LORD continually (Exodus 28:29)

The Biblical language about names and signs implies that each of the twelve stones of the *ephod* symbolizes a particular quality that every individual member of each family must carry, and thus, the acceptance and understanding of one's dreams is truly, each person's own responsibility.

In a dream, in a vision of the night, when deep sleep falleth upon men, in slumberings upon the bed; Then he openeth the ears of men, and sealeth their instruction (Job 33:15-16).

Specifically, the Bible says that God speaks to each person, individually in dreams and visions:

The LORD said suddenly to Moses, to Aaron, and to Miriam, "You three go out to the Tent of Meeting." And the three of them went out. The LORD came down in a pillar of cloud and stood in the opening to the Tent, and he called Aaron and Miriam: the two of them went out. He said, Hear now my words: If there shall be prophets among you, in a vision shall I the LORD make myself known to him, in a dream shall I speak to him. Not so is my servant Moses; in my entire house he is the trusted one. Mouth to mouth do I speak to him, in a clear vision and not in dark speeches, at the image of the Lord does he gaze (Numbers 12:1-9).

Here is the clear distinction between visions and dreams. Aaron, the High priest and wearer of the Breast Piece of Judgment, is the same as any other man or woman. God speaks to him, the High priest, and to his sister, Miriam, just as he speaks to every other person: in dreams and visions of the night. Only to their brother Moses does God speak mouth to mouth, or face to face. The Hebrew word *peh* used here means both mouth and face. The Talmud explains that Moses sees God in a clear bright mirror, while everyone else looks into a dim distorted glass.

PERSONAL DREAMS

Adam asleep is the first sleep in the Bible. Adam is totally unconscious of dreaming and, in fact, experiences his dream as real, or perhaps as a waking dream. is The first truly instructive dream in the Bible is Abimelech's dream in Genesis 20.

These are the events that preceded Abimelech's dream. Sodom and Gomorrah had been destroyed. Abraham's nephew Lot had escaped the destruction of those cities with his wife and two daughters. Lot's wife had been warned not to look back to the sin filled cities of Sodom and Gomorrah; nevertheless, she did look back, and was turned into a pillar of salt. Lot and his daughters took shelter in a cave. Lot's daughters, fearing that there were no men left on earth to continue the human race, decided to make their father drunk, and to lie with him so that he would impregnate them and repopulate the earth. Soon afterward, perhaps disgusted with these goings on, Abraham decides to leave this area. The story continues...

> And Abraham journeyed from thence toward the south country, and dwelled between Kadesh and Shur, and sojourned in Gerar. And Abraham said of Sarah his wife, She is my sister: and Abimelech king of Gerar sent, and took Sarah. But God came to Abimelech in a dream by night, and said to him, Behold, thou art but a dead man, for the woman which thou hast taken; for she is a man's wife (Genesis 20:1-4).

When the Bible says God came to Abimelech in a dream, the Hebrew word "came" used here in Genesis 20:3 is not the same as saying that God appeared to Abimelech in a dream. Later, in the Bible both Laban and Balaam like Abimelech, say that God came to them. When God appeared or revealed himself to Moses as the burning bush the Hebrew word *v'eira*, made himself be seen, or appeared himself, is used. Moses actually sees God. When God says I make myself known to him in a vision; I speak to him in a dream (Numbers 12:6) the expression *m'arot Elohim* or visions of God is used. The verb see is the root of both *m'arot* and *v'eira*. The word *d'aber*, "spoke," which is used when God spoke to the patriarchs, is not used either. Therefore the traditional understanding by Sforno and others is that the *voice* of God came to Abimelech in a dream. This is a less compelling experience than seeing God, and Abimelech is able to argue with the voice in the dream. This first dream in the Bible is truly instructive. The voice of God, or intuition which the Gnostics called inner knowledge, came to Abimelech and saved his life.

In the dream Abimelech hears God say that he is a dead man, asleep, unconscious; the woman he has taken is the wife of a husband. In the earlier incident when Abraham said that Sarah was his sister, he had done so because he was afraid that the men of the place would kill him in order to take Sarah from him and possess her. In that time, and in that place, the prohibition against intercourse with another man's wife was observed zealously. A man would sooner murder the husband in order to be free to possess the man's wife, than break the taboo against committing adultery. The inner voice that told Abimelech that Sarah was a man's wife saved Abimelech's life and, we learn later, the lives of all the future generations of his people.

> But Abimelech had not come near her: and he said, Lord, wilt thou slay also a righteous nation? Said he not unto me, She is my sister? and she, even she herself said, He is my brother: in the integrity of my heart and innocency of my hands have I done this. And God said unto him in a dream, Yea, I know that thou didst this in the integrity of thy heart; for I also withheld thee from sinning against me: therefore suffered I thee not to touch her (Genesis 20:4-7).

Abimelech argues that he has not yet approached her. He asks, *"Will you slay a nation along with a righteous one?"* If he, Abimelech, a righteous man and King dies, his nation will die also. Or perhaps Abimelech means that if he and his people die because of Abraham's lie, both a nation and Abraham, a righteous one, will die.

While there is nothing in the Bible story to indicate that Abimelech had doubted that Sarah was Abraham's sister, in the dream he says *"And she, too, herself said. . ."* Abimelech had suspected Abraham's story; something in him had required Sarah's assurance as well. The word for "too," *gam*, is an extension and implies the others: Sarah, her ass drivers, her camel drivers, her domestics, and all her household said that Abraham was her brother. Despite what both Abraham and Sarah and her entourage had said, something had prevented Abimelech from making love to her.

Some say that an angel prevented Abimelech from intercourse with Sarah by stealing his desire and rendering him impotent. He says. "In the innocence of my heart and, literally, the cleanness of my hands have I done this. And God said to him in the dream, 'I, too, knew that it was in the innocence of your heart that you did this, and I, too, prevented you from sinning against me. That is why I did not permit you, literally, *give* you the ability to touch her." The *Midrash* comments: It is like the case of a warrior who is riding his horse at full speed when he sees a child in the road. He reigns in his horse so the child is not hurt. Whom do we praise: the horse or the rider? Surely the reigning in came from the inner voice of intuition or the higher Self.

The voice of God continues in the dream: *"But now return the man's wife for he is a prophet"* (Genesis 20:8). This is the first time the word prophet appears in the Bible. The word for prophet, *nevi*, is related to the phrase *"expressions of the lips"* (Isaiah 57:19). It means one who is frequently near God and speaks his teaching. It is not the function of a prophet to foretell the future. That is incidental to his primary function, which is to be the vessel and the organ through which God's will reaches mankind. The voice in the dream repeats saying literally, *"And if you do not restore her, die, you shall surely die."* Repetition within a dream, like a recurrent dream, adds emphasis, insists upon attention and compliance. This dream of Abimelech's is a fine example of how a dream can highlight what a person only senses intuitively. Abimelech listened attentively to its instruction:

> Therefore Abimelech rose early in the morning, and called all his servants, and told all these things in their ears: and the men were sore afraid. Then Abimelech called Abraham, and said unto him, What hast thou done unto us? and what have I offended thee, that thou hast brought on me and on my kingdom a great sin? thou hast done deeds unto me that ought not to be done. And Abimelech said

unto Abraham, What sawest thou, that thou hast done this thing? And Abraham said, Because I thought, Surely the fear of God is not in this place; and they will slay me for my wife's sake. And yet indeed she is my sister; she is the daughter of my father, but not the daughter of my mother; and she became my wife. And it came to pass, when God caused me to wander from my father's house, that I said unto her, This is thy kindness which thou shalt shew unto me; at every place whither we shall come, say of me, He is my brother (Genesis 20:8-14).

Abimelech heeds his dreamwork. He asks, "What was it about me that made you lie to me and put me and my people in such danger? What did you see in me that made you think that I would kill you, or rape your wife?" Despite the lameness of Abraham's explanation of how Sarah is technically also his sister, Abimelech follows the instructions given him in the dream.

Abimelech does all he can to make restitution to both Abraham and Sarah. He deeply believes that full restitution is needed to obtain Abraham's prayers:

And Abimelech took sheep, and oxen, and menservants, and women servants, and gave them unto Abraham, and restored him Sarah his wife. And Abimelech said, Behold, my land is before thee: dwell where it pleaseth thee. And unto Sarah he said, Behold, I have given thy brother a thousand pieces of silver: behold, he is to thee a covering of the eyes, unto all that are with thee, and with all other: thus she was reproved. So Abraham prayed unto God: and God healed Abimelech, and his wife, and his maidservants; and they bare children. For the LORD had fast closed up all the wombs of the house of Abimelech, because of Sarah Abraham's wife (Genesis 20:14-19).

By listening attentively to his dream, Abimelech and his entire nation were saved. The name *Abimelech*, in Hebrew, means "father of kings." By taking seriously the dream instruction to return Sarah to her husband, Abimelech became more truly himself, father of kings. And incidentally, Abraham too, became a father very soon thereafter. Immediately in the next passage of the Bible:

> The LORD remembered Sarah as he had said; and the LORD did for Sarah as he had spoken. Sarah conceived and bore a son unto Abraham in his old age (Genesis 21:1).

Like the ripple effect of a pebble thrown into a puddle, when one person listens to the divine instruction given to him in dreams, in some mysterious and subtle way, everyone close to the dreamer benefits as well.

WITHOUT A DREAM

> *Blue moon*
> *You saw me standing alone*
> *Without a dream in my heart*
> *Without a love of my own**

The popular definition of "Once in a Blue Moon" is the second full moon in a calendar month; it occurs about once every two and a half years. The older more traditional meaning of the Blue Moon is the third Full Moon in a season which has four Full Moons. This third full moon was shown in the Farmer's Almanac in blue. Hence the name.

The Blue Moon of the song speaks to both the unusualness of the occurrence, the feeling of loneliness to be without a dream, and most of all, to the magic of the moon seeing what a human needs. The Zohar speaks of both the Shekhina and Lilith as having been born from the diminishment of the moon. For me, the Blue Moon has always carried the meaning of the Shekhina who also brings dreams and the terrible sense of estrangement and loss when there are no dreams, and no love. The loneliness of no love, and no dreams in the face of terrible fear is described in the Bible:

And when Saul saw the host of the Philistines, he was afraid, and

---

© Rogers and Hart, 1934.

his heart greatly trembled. And when Saul enquired of the LORD, the LORD answered him not, neither by dreams, nor by Urim, nor by prophets (I Samuel 28:5-7).

Dream deprived, alienated from the Self, lost and abandoned Saul sent for the Witch of Endor. She in turn told him to ask the High Priest Samuel for help.

And Samuel said to Saul, Why hast thou disquieted me, to bring me up? And Saul answered, I am sore distressed; for the Philistines make war against me, and God is departed from me, and answereth me no more, neither by prophets, nor by dreams: therefore I have called thee, that thou mayest make known unto me what I shall do. Then said Samuel, Wherefore then dost thou ask of me, seeing the LORD is departed from thee (I Samuel 28:15-17).

Saul, precisely because he feels abandoned by God, abandons God. He does not pray, or dream. Neither the Witch of Endor, nor the High Priest can make for Saul the direct connection to God that he needs. A personal, conscious awareness one's own need is required, and a personal direct prayer to God in any language is required. Saul does not pray.

Saul, abandoned and abandoning God, suffers this fate:

And it came to pass on the morrow, when the Philistines came to strip the slain, that they found Saul and his three sons fallen in mount Gilboa. And they cut off his head, and stripped off his armour, and sent into the land of the Philistines round about, to publish it in the house of their idols, and among the people. And they put his armour in the house of Ashtaroth: and they fastened his body to the wall of Bethshan (I Samuel 31:8-11).

Interestingly enough, Ashtaroth too, was a Moon Goddess, but Saul did not pray to her either. He had no love and no faith, suffered the terrible loss, and died from it. In the end he fell upon his own sword. All through his life Saul was plagued with black depressions, and murderous rages. God had truly departed from him. Reb Nachman says that it is the *Yetzer ha-Ra,* the evil impulse, that tells us that God has departed, and that one must not accept that voice. But how can we humanly suffer and transform that feeling? How can we experience and not die from the loss of faith, connection, rage and despair when we feel that God and the Shekhina have departed from us?

When one suffers a blue moon time—a time when one is away from God, a time when one is alone, without a dream in your heart, and without a love of your own—then one feels abandoned by God. When God goes, so does love.

It is then when one is sick with love, or need of love that the lover's annunciation in the Song of Songs is relevant. At a certain point in the narrative of the Song of Songs, when the time is right, her soul awakened, the female lover announces:

Hark! my beloved! behold, he comes leaping upon the mountains, bounding over the hills. Look there he stands behind our wall, looking through the windows, peering through the lattice (Song of Songs 2:9).

She suddenly feels a possibility. She is partially seen by her lover. He is hidden by the wall. and she does not really see him either. The Song of Songs speaks of "our" wall. It is certainly a wall that we put up. A wall of fear, distrust, coldness, forgetfulness, or any of the hundred other things—drugs, alcohol, and acting out—that can be used to create a barrier. The verse speaks of three barriers between the lover and the beloved. First, he stands behind a wall. Then he gazes through a window. Lastly, he peers through a lattice. These barriers allow different degrees of hiding between lovers, and between us and God.

A barrier may also be used protectively to create a safe haven, or to increase focus and concentration, or to create a frame and add perspective. Muslim and Orthodox Jewish men and women pray separately. In Orthodox Jewish houses of prayer men and women are separated by a *mehchitza,* or lattice work barrier, so that they do not lose their connection to God by being distracted by fantasies of the lover or beloved.

These barriers are also put up between lovers, and between a person and God. We need to understand that they are our walls, our defensive walls erected in early life even before we have words or understanding. When hurt or fearful we quickly learn to withdraw and to hide behind a wall of unconsciousness. One feels alone and bereft.

Suddenly the soul awakes and announces: this wall is merely a lattice work. There is an opening and God is here just behind the lattice.

The Rabbis spoke of this verse of the Song of Songs as showing that God is often very close to someone in need, and that if only they could recognize and lower the barrier of distrust, or lost faith, and disappointment they would feel the full experience of the loving divine presence. In both human and transpersonal relationships barriers and limitations are sometimes necessary, and sometimes wreak havoc. Praying or wishing for a dream and soulful dreamwork brings healing and renewal.

Love and Fear

And thou shalt love the LORD thy God with all thine heart, and with all thy soul, and with all thy might

  and

Thou shalt love thy neighbour as thyself: I am the LORD.

These are two of the most well-known commandments. If you really love God there is no room for fear in your heart, when fear is gone, so is hate. There is no reason to think that being "spiritual" is being alone in solitary confinement. Indeed the best peace, says Reb Nachman, is the peace between opposites. This idea chooses me. Makes me wonder. It makes me ask, as the Mussar Hasids do, what is it that my little animal soul needs and wants? It is being at "one." Inner marriage is being ONE. It is being fully one's self, or being one with God. Love thy neighbor as thyself is clear: Self love is basic. Only then, can one truly love an other.

The Baal Shem Tov, the founder of Chassidism, taught that what you see in others is what you are yourself. When you feel angry with another person you need to ask yourself, "Where is that trait, the thing that makes me angry with my neighbor—where is that in me?" In dreams the person who is the same sex as the dreamer, but is not the dreamer, is the shadow on whom rests the unlived or unacceptable traits and actions of the dreamer. If one does soulful dreamwork, and makes the effort to relate to the Other, and, if one truly listens with an open heart and responds honestly and fully from the heart, this process of integration proceeds, and wholeness happens!

Jung and other psychoanalysts say the same thing. Each of us needs to integrate our own shadow. When you are critical of another it is always worthwhile to ask yourself "What is it in myself that I see and despise in the other?"

Orthodox Jews believe that each of us struggle within with the two conflicting impulses, the *Yetzer ha Ra* and the *Yetzer ha Tov*, the impulse toward evil and the impulse toward good. For Rabbi Nachman himself the *Yetzer ha Ra* took the form of a terrible pull toward depression. He wrote often that this was the Evil One's attempt to keep one from being close to God, and he advised people to fight strenuously against this pull toward depression.

When the Jewish people left *Mizriam*, or the narrow enslavement of Egypt, they did not go directly to Mount Sinai and receive the Torah. They had to prepare themselves and learn what their strengths were, and what their bad habits were. They had to take serious stock of themselves. They had to learn to be free human beings. Soulful dreamwork is the most direct and personally responsible way to do this. When one is fully human, and free, out of Eden, one must be responsible for, and integrate one's own shadow.

The Talmud (Tanchuma, Bereshit I) says that the Torah was written on white fire, with black fire. Rabbi Nachman taught that the *Yetzer ha Ra* or the evil inclination can be used not only as an impetus for sin, but as a passion for *mitzvoth*, or following the commandments as well. The black fire, the fire of the *Yetzer ha Ra*, can and must be used to write on the white fire of the *Yetzer ha Tov*, the good inclination. Without the passion of the black fire, the white fire is blank and devoid of any divine message telling us what we can and must do. The Torah could not be written with white fire alone, nor can human beings exist without having a shadow. Psychologically, one must integrate the black fire of one's shadow to be authentic, whole and three dimensional.

LETTING GO

A woman who was depressed, angry and withdrawn as a result of having some health problems associated with aging dreamt that she had said to her son who was half her age, "Let's do something wild." Then she'd suggested that they go to a movie. Her son was very disappointed and annoyed with her. When the dialogue continued as an active imagination, her son said that action was required—real fire, not just the passive projections of watching a movie. The woman saw that she was angry with God for having abandoned her. She had always felt that she was a "lucky duck," a favorite of God, and recent events, terrible losses, death and heath problems had made her feel "wild" with anger and black fire. Her young energetic son personified a form of heroic leadership and forward-moving energy. The dream made her take up the task of Self knowing, again.

Letting go has been a familiar mantra for this woman. Intuition, imagination, speed, originality, and passion have fired her. Menopause released her from the wheel of life. She was surprised to find that when her lunar cycles ceased she felt, not loss, but a delightful wave of "post menopausal zest," to steal a phrase from Margaret Mead.

From the time she was a child, this woman had always believed herself to be a "lucky duck." When she was in her sixties, she had a series of dreams: a dead duck, a chicken, a dream of making an offering of the lucky duck. And then she dreamt:

> I was walking into my town Library with the peacock blue bird in my arms when it flew off and perched in a nearby tree. A woman came out of the library and I asked her if she knew how to "handle" a bird. She said "why"? Meaning why handle it? "Why" is the wrong question. I agreed. Let it go. And I did.

The woman wrote in her dream journal:

> That blue peacock was gorgeous, but holding on to it was like holding on to a narcissistic need to be seen, look good, to "handle" things well . . . . None of this feels good any more. . . . Letting go is the mantra of my '60s. . . . I like the simplicity of this, the minimalist approach. It appealed to me aesthetically, and emotionally. The secret pleasure of age I have found, is this tremendous sense of freedom and joy.

Both the Lucky Duck, and Blue Peacock are shadow elements for this woman. Her soulful dreamwork helped her know and integrate these aspects of her self.

I AM BLACK BUT COMELY

> I am black but comely, O you daughters of Jerusalem . . . as the tents
> of Kedar . . . as the curtains of Solomon (Song of Songs I:5).

The beloved in the Song of Songs has fallen from her exalted state of joy
into a depressed state of nomadic wandering in the desert wilderness. She
continues,

> Take no notice of my swarthiness. It is the sun that has burnt me.
> My mother's sons were incensed against me. They made me keeper
> of the vine yards. Had I only looked after my own (Song of Songs
> I:5-7).

The beloved Shulamite has been blackened by the sun, or the super
rational, exacting, solar value system of her mother's sons. This happens
psychologically when a girl has been burnt by her mother's unconscious critical angry attitude toward her. Often when such a daughter falls in love she
is brought close to this experience of being burnt. In just this state a woman
dreamt:

> *I am talking to my dark cousin . . . black, but comely . . . comes to mind. She was not
> with us in the bad times, but she clearly had had her own bad time. She was born in the
> same year I was just on the brink of the Second World War, but in a world of Eastern
> Europe full of political upheaval and under the dark sun of the Nazi scourge, while I
> was born into the light hopeful new world in America, secure, with my darkness inside.
> While we share our stories we see first, a body on a green iridescent couch. Later, we see
> the same body in an office on an analyst's couch.*

The dreamer said:

> *I feel that somehow the outer world, where I will give papers, and where my lover lives,
> and my inner world of need and longing, will coalesce. He will find a way to be with me.
> I am learning about my history with him. I am learning about inner and outer worlds.
> I am learning about upper and lower, and past and future . . .*

Indeed, the dreamer was engaged in a process of soulful dreamwork and Self discovery. Like the black Shulamite she understood the causes of her blackened state, and she had similar regrets.

The state of imperfect transformation is one of sad alienation from the Self, great loneliness, and black despair, but just when one is about to give up, the blessed green of hope of Spring and renewal appears. For this dreamer the body and the bed are iridescent with hope and life.

The beloved Shulamite, in her depressed and blackened state, does not want to go on wandering like the nomadic people of Kedar, descendants of outcast Ishmael, in her blackened and veiled state like a harlot (Genesis 38:15) or a leper (Leviticus 13:45).

The tents of the nomadic Bedouin are woven from the hair of black goats and are black, but the Hebrew root word, *kdr,* itself carries the idea of darkness and is used to describe the darkness of an eclipse of the sun or the moon (Joel 2:10, 4:15; Micah 3:6). It is used also to mean the darkening of storm clouds (Jeremiah 4:28) and of a turbid stream (Job 6:16). The same word for dark is used to describe mourning garb (Jeremiah 8:21, 14:2; Job 5:11, 30:28; Psalms 35:14, 38:7, 42:10, 43:2) In the soulful language of dreams these are all emotional states of abandonment, desolation, loss and depression.

While the tents of Kedar express the outer darkness and protective shelter, the curtains of Solomon provide an inner secret place. It is sometimes necessary to stay in retreat within the blackened state and in connection with the secret inner underlying blessed greenness. These are the curtains that surround and set off the mystery of the holy of holies and create a dwelling place for the Shekhina.

Her lover tells her:

If you do not know, most beautiful of women, follow in the footsteps of the sheep and graze your young goats by the dwelling places of the shepherds (Song of Songs 1:8-9).

Indeed the Shulamite does not know herself. She has just now discovered her plight of self betrayal. She understands that she has lived by a false value system—that of her mother's sons, or some other psychologically damaging misunderstanding or unconsciousness. Therefore, she does need to learn a new way of looking after her younger self, or her new and vulnerable young kids. Her lover, unlike her mother's sons, does not exploit her. He says instead, "Follow in the footsteps of those that have gone before you." Since the beloved's personal experience has been so painful she needs now to find her own way in the world.

A woman whose early history was difficult because her mother was so narcissistic suffered a dreadful envious attack from two women in her dream group. She wrote in her journal,

> *I can no longer share my dreams with these devouring females. . . . I recall a dream from years before . . . they are so like the fat lesbians masturbating with a furry animal trapped in a stocking in the dream cave of the night mother. . . . I must go on my inner way alone . . . at one with myself.*

That night she dreamt of entering a candlelit, luminous, golden-red holy place that was the place of the Shekhina. She was not alone.

IN A DREAM, IN A VISION OF THE NIGHT

There was a man in the land of Uz, whose name was Job; and that man was perfect and upright, and one that feared God, and eschewed evil. And there were born unto him seven sons and three daughters. His substance also was seven thousand sheep, and three thousand camels, and five hundred yoke of oxen, and five hundred she asses, and a very great household; so that this man was the greatest of all the men of the east (Job I:1-7).

And suddenly, in a devastating sequence Job lost his seven sons, his three daughters, his sheep, his camels, his oxen, asses, and household servants.

Despite this calamity, Job kept his faith in God's goodness. He did not complain of God's will. Then his friends arrived to comfort Job. They sat with him for an entire week, but did not speak. After this Job opened his mouth. He began to say that he wished he had never been born. One of Job's comforters, a friend close enough to seem an inner voice, asks Job if he is sure that he is entirely innocent. He suggests that since God is all good, Job must have sinned to have such bad things happen to him. He tells Job his dream, or perhaps merely a night thought:

> Now a thing was secretly brought to me, and mine ear received a little thereof. In thoughts from the visions of the night, when deep sleep falleth on men Fear came upon me, and trembling, which made all my bones to shake. Then a spirit passed before my face; the hair of my flesh stood up: It stood still, but I could not discern the form thereof: an image was before mine eyes, there was silence, and I heard a voice, saying, Shall mortal man be more just than God? shall a man be more pure than his maker? (Job 4:12-18).

A tiny crack of self doubt opens in Job. His comforter makes a good case for these terrible losses are God's correction for possible sins committed by Job. He argues that God must be just, so Job must admit to being bad and deserving of God's punishment.

But Job does not feel that he has sinned and he suffers the conflict inwardly: He feels poisoned by the events of his life. He wishes that God would allow him to die. He expects justice from God.

Job believes the nights should comfort him, but Job has no dreams: he rides the night mare:

> Wearisome nights are appointed to me. When I lie down, I say, When shall I arise, and the night be gone? and I am full of tossings to and fro unto the dawning of the day (Job 7:1-7).

In anguish, Job cries out,

> Therefore I will not refrain my mouth; I will speak in the anguish of my spirit; I will complain in the bitterness of my soul. Am I a

sea, or a whale, that thou settest a watch over me? When I say, My bed shall comfort me, my couch shall ease my complaint; Then thou scarest me with dreams, and terrifiest me through visions: So that my soul chooseth strangling, and death rather than my life. I loathe it; I would not live always: let me alone; for my days are vanity (Job 7:11-17).

And, here, finally, Job begins to talk with God. This dialogue is more personal than Moses' dialogue with God. Job asks the central question: What does God need from man?

What is man, that thou shouldest magnify him? and that thou shouldest set thine heart upon him? And that thou shouldest visit him every morning, and try him every moment? How long wilt thou not depart from me, nor let me alone till I swallow down my spittle? I have sinned; what shall I do unto thee, O thou preserver of men? why hast thou set me as a mark against thee, so that I am a burden to myself? And why dost thou not pardon my transgression, and take away mine iniquity? For now shall I sleep in the dust; and thou shalt seek me in the morning, but I shall not be (Job 7:17-22).

Clearly Job still believes that God is just and that his suffering is payment for some transgression. When another one of Job's comforters suggests that it was the *children* of Job who have sinned and that if Job would point this out to God, God would restore Job to his former wealth. Job however, cannot reason with God: As we often do, Job takes the blame for his hardship upon himself, and feels sad and depressed. He says,

My soul is weary of my life; I will leave my complaint upon myself; I will speak in the bitterness of my soul. I will say unto God, Do not condemn me; shew me wherefore thou contendest with me (Job 10:1-3).

Finally Job dismisses his comforters saying,

But ye are forgers of lies, ye are all physicians of no value. (Job 13:4) ... miserable comforters are ye all (Job 16:2) ... thou hast made desolate all my company. And thou hast filled me with wrinkles... (Job 16:9).

After having listened to the three so-called comforters, after much reasoning and debate, much blame, and their alienating inadequate advice, a fourth comforter, much younger than the others, and very angry, emerges:

So these three men ceased to answer Job, because he was righteous in his own eyes. Then was kindled the wrath of Elihu the son of Barachel the Buzite, of the kindred of Ram: against Job was his wrath kindled, because he justified himself rather than God. Also against his three friends was his wrath kindled, because they had found no answer, and yet had condemned Job (Job 32:1-4).

The fire-filled fourth comforter says to Job:

There is no teacher like God, For God speaketh once, yea twice, yet man perceiveth it not. *In a dream, in a vision of the night, when deep sleep falleth upon men, in slumberings upon the bed; Then he openeth the ears of men, and sealeth their instruction,* that he may withdraw man from his purpose, and hide pride from man. He keepeth back his soul from the pit, and his life from perishing by the sword (Job 33:14-19).

What does God need from man? Finally, from God comes this astonishing answer to Job, in the form of a question:

Who is this that darkeneth counsel by words without knowledge? Gird up now thy loins like a man; for I will demand of thee, and answer thou me.

Where wast thou when I laid the foundations of the earth? declare, if thou hast understanding. Who hath laid the measures thereof, if thou knowest? or who hath stretched the line upon it? Whereupon are the foundations thereof fastened? or who laid the corner stone thereof? When the morning stars sang together, and all the sons of God shouted for joy? Or who shut up the sea with doors, when it brake forth, as if it had issued out of the womb? When I made the cloud the garment thereof, and thick darkness a swaddlingband for it, And brake up for it my decreed place, and set bars and doors ... (Job 38:1-11).

Job was not there when God laid the foundations of the earth. It was Wisdom, *Sophia*, who says:

The LORD possessed me in the beginning of his way, before his works of old. I was set up from everlasting, from the beginning, or ever the earth was. When there were no depths, I was brought forth; when there were no fountains abounding with water. Before the mountains were settled, before the hills was I brought forth: While as yet he had not made the earth, nor the fields, nor the highest part of the dust of the world. When he prepared the heavens, I was there: when he set a compass upon the face of the depth: When he established the clouds above: when he strengthened the fountains of the deep: When he gave to the sea his decree, that the waters should not pass his commandment: when he appointed the foundations of the earth: Then I was by him, as one brought up with him: and I was daily his delight, rejoicing always before him (Proverbs 8:22-30).

Wisdom was with God in those days of creation. It is this knowing companionship that God requires from Job. It is this partner in creation that God needs. This is God's answer to Job's question, "Why have you set your heart upon human beings?" God needs man, and man needs God. In a dream, in a vision of the night, God will open the ears of human beings, and instruct them. Together, doing soulful dreamwork, man and God co-create and continue the world.

PART THREE

Integration

Salt

There are two parts to my work. The part I have written about and the most important part: the part I can never write about, because it is the dream itself. This is the wordless experience of meaning. The soul dancing in time and memory. It is the flash of intuitive inner knowing, and the flood of memory and connection that comes with *knowing* what the dream means.

$\sim$

At the end of the year there was Christmas at the weekend, and New Years at the other end of a week. It was a seven day period of reflection and then: a Tsunami. The earth shifted, the sea roiled, and a tidal wave swept away thousands of lives.

A friend told me this: She had been feeling her sixty-sixth year as a year of transition. A popular song from her childhood, "Get Your Kicks on Route Sixty-Six," played in the background of her mind. She was on her own for the first time ever. No parents, no husband, no children, no lover at the center, in fact no center at all other than a questing spirit of *hitbedout*, aloneness fueled by inward joy and freedom! She felt often the poetic intention of Amichai's words:

> Like high mountain climbers who set up a base in the valley at the
> foot of the mountains and another camp and camp number two and
> camp number three at various heights on the road to the peak . . .
> so I leave my childhood and my youth and my adult years in vari-
> ous camps with a flag on every camp. I know I shall never return,
> but to get to the peak with no weight, light, light (Yehuda Amichai,
> "Life").

At the beginning of the year she had ended a long love affair that was weighing her down. Just before the days of Awe between Rosh ha Shana and Yom Kippur—when people reflect on themselves and do a process of *teshuva*, a return to their true selves or God—her former lover came to see her. They talked for the first time since they had parted and she was relieved of the burden of sadness that she had carried. Weight began to fall off her. She had to buy new clothes, returning to a size she had worn thirty years earlier, and she stopped writing. She was feeling that poetic blank, the pause. No thing. No words. Silent. Inside. Happy. Then, as the year darkened, the green died, and she felt the loss, and the tears fell.

At Chanukah, when she was in the country, feeling cold on a rainy day, a *midrash* came to her from a friend. Her friend had imagined what it was to find a very small flask of oil, intact, dusty, old, even ancient, but unbroken and a survivor after all the anger and destruction of war. The oil within, poured out, and lit with a spark, flames into light and warmth. The little flask of oil contained only a few drops of oil, but it was enough, *dayenu*, a miracle. The year turned, and friends and family returned from distant time and places. They brought gifts of stories and heart.

Almost immediately a man whom she called the love of her life telephoned her. A year had passed since his wife died. And a year had passed since her parting from her lover. For the first time in their twenty-year-long relationship they were both free. The woman said:

He asked me to come and live with him. He asked me to marry him. I do not want to leave my work here, I told him. He asked if he could come and live with me. He can leave his University and come to me. He remembers our time together here with me and our remarkable meetings over the years. Then, we were bound to place and time by work, children, vows, and bound to each other by love. All love is memory of love he told me then. No, I thought, not all. But then I did not know the meaning of time....

Now, I said, let us have some time. A long weekend, a long week, a long summer month's stay. Let us try your place, my place, and a traveling place. Time and place are easy now. Very soon we were together in place for five days at Valentine's time. Time and memory and place were there, love was there, but now there was a terrible gulf. He is sick, and I am well. The unbridgeable gulf he tells me, is not between man and woman, or black and white, or good and bad. These all find a third way or a bridge. The unbridgeable gulf, he says, is between the sick and the well. He is very very ill.

Time with me was always an adventure, a bit wild, he told me. He wants to remember us like that, not with me as his nurse. He wants to live with me he says, not because he wants me to take care of him, but because he loves me. He wants to marry me. He will not come to me if he is sick. I left a note on his pillow saying, "This was the best time we have ever had together, and the most terrible. All my love. ..." And I flew home.

She went to the country place where long ago they had once spent a month together in glorious green summer. It was cold and dark now. She felt alone, an orphan and a widow driving home from the country, dark and cold, alone, no God. Then the woman said:

I dreamt of giant Tarot cards. I was placing them, one over the other, on an angle, this way and that, face down, not looking at them. Fateful. This makes the blind widow who lives in my house angry. She warns me, "Again," she says. "Time," she says. I see that I am afraid. I fear surviving. The gulf that separates the healthy from the sick is enormous.

She wrote to her beloved, "I want to be your person. Let us be together in whatever way we can be."

She dreamt:

A salad had been made. "Mrs. Kennedy" throws a handful of kosher salt onto it, and all at once, it comes alive!

The widow Kennedy, the widow Onassis, throws a handful of kosher salt, and transforms inert blackness into blessed greenness.

He who works without salt will never raise dead bodies (Jung, *Mysterium Coniunctionis*, 245).

Jung writes about the black Shulamite in the Song of Songs who suffers loss, loneliness, and seclusion. She is "alone among the hidden" but nevertheless she has rejoice in my heart: "Under my blackness I have hidden the fairest green."

The state of imperfect transformation . . . does not seem to be one of torment only, but of positive if hidden, happiness. It is the state of someone who, in his wanderings among the mazes of his psychic transformation, comes upon a secret happiness which reconciles him to his apparent loneliness. In communing with himself he finds not deadly boredom and melancholy but an inner partner . . . a relationship that seems like the happiness of a secret love, or like a hidden springtime, when the green seed sprouts from the barren earth . . . . Green signifies hope and the future, and herein lies the reason for the Shulamite's hidden joy. . . .The sense of blackness merely covering a much deeper rich life force occurs frequently in psychic and spiritual life (C. G. Jung, *Mysterium Coniunctionis*, 432).

The widow Kennedy, the widow Onassis, does not merely come upon the blessed greenness. She herself, with full intention, throws a handful of kosher salt, and that is what brings the blessed greenness into life. Salt can do that, salt tears flow and wisdom comes, or salt can harden and become bitter. Lot's wife looks back, even after being warned "Do not look back," and she becomes forever fixed, a pillar of salt. Mrs. Kennedy takes herself in hand, moves forward, loves again. She does not marry again, she is not constricted by the past, fixed forever in hard bitter form.

My friend says,

The first marriage [of Jacqueline Bouvier] was for convention, love and children. There was not much love, two dead children, and two live children. The second marriage was for protection, a needed residue from the first. And the last—not a marriage, but a feeling of soul connection—to a Jewish financier who gave her both freedom and love.

Then she copied into her dream journal the essay she had recalled:

I saw a woman sleeping. In her sleep she dreamt Life stood before her, and held in each hand a gift—in the one Love, in the other Freedom. And she said to the woman, "Choose!"

And the woman waited long: and she said, "Freedom!"

And Life said, "Thou hast well chosen. If thou hadst said, 'Love,' I would have given Thee that thou didst ask for; and I would have gone from Thee, and returned to thee no more. Now,

the day will come when I shall return. In that day I shall bear both gifts in one hand."
I heard the woman laugh in her sleep.
(Olive Schreiner, *Life's Gifts*, 1890)

These nights my friend dreams of the circle becoming square and a sense of completion.

> Just as the world soul pervades all things, so does salt. ... It repre-
> sents the feminine principle of Eros, which brings everything into
> relationship, in an almost perfect way.... The sign for salt was origi-
> nally ⊡—a double totality symbol, the circle representing non-
> differentiated wholeness, and the square discriminated wholeness.
> (C. G. Jung, *Mysterium Coniunctionis*, 241).

Jung tells us that the most outstanding properties of salt are bitterness and wisdom. What holds these two properties together is *feeling*. Tears, sorrow, and disappointment are bitter; wisdom is the comfort for all psychic suffering. Bitterness and wisdom can be seen as alternatives: "where there is bitterness wisdom is lacking, and where wisdom is there can be no bitterness" (*Mysterium Coniunctionis*, 247).

The salt of the earth is the soul. The *anima mundi*. The Queen of Sheba, she who loves wisdom, travels to Jerusalem to find the wise man and becomes her Self, *Sophia*, wisdom. The widow, and the white dove, feminine wisdom and partner of God? The soul of the earth—the Shekhina?

A Guide for the Perplexed

Once upon a time there was a woman who was lost and depressed. There was no thing that interested her and no thing to do. There was no thing to look forward to. Then the woman who was lost dreamt:

I am in a house of dolchi, sweetness. It is not my house. I have been here before but now I am lost and confused. Is this all new? How does it fit together? What is my place here?

All thru the night there was another dream motif: I am trying to devise a way that a mouse would "fall thru" an unrolled swath of saffron colored cloth, and the person, me, running along the same path of cloth held aloft would escape the trap. My solution was to make a + cut in the cloth, but of course the little mouse would fall thru, but when I got there, I too would fall thru. Over and over again, I saw the flaw in my attempts to deal with the problem, but I remained perplexed.

When the woman wrote the dream in her journal she immediately saw the "joke": "I know the mouse is that instinctive little sexual tickle that makes pubescent girls and women shriek." The problem of the dream is how to let the mouse go without falling through into an emotional place herself. The house of sweetness was a place where the wife tolerated her husband's frequent infidelities in exchange for "the sweet life" style. These two ways cross each other. There is the inner way of the Self, the saffron colored cloth, and the outer way of the house of too much, of the too sweet life style.

The mystic way of the alchemist seeking the Philosopher's Stone is to turn inward for the voyage; despite all the alchemist's arts, he will not find the stone in "foreign parts"—outside of the Self.

Or, neither, in the outer way of acting out, and falling into the simple instinctual hole and trap. The woman realized that she could keep herself away from the small + cross, or the imagined plus of a simply sexual solution, by staying back, away from the place where the mouse fell through, and choosing to exercise Self control.

The woman thought of an aphorism of the seventeenth-century German mystic, Angelus Silesius: "God is my center when I close him in, And my circumference when I melt in him

She opened the Torah portion for that week (it was a Saturday morning) and found that it was about observing Shabbat. This often happens. When there is great need, and an open questing spirit, and a listening heart, the answers come synchronistically.

The *Torah* portion read:

> Six days shall work be done, but on the seventh day there shall be to you a holy day, a Sabbath of rest to the LORD: whosoever doeth work therein shall be put to death (Exodus 35:2).

The Hebrew word, *melacha*, "work," used here is the same word used to describe the work of building the Tabernacle. It seemed extraordinary to the sages that God who is infinite, all powerful and everywhere should need man to make a place for God to dwell on earth. They wrote:

> When the Holy One Blessed be He said to Moses "Make for Me a *Mikdash*," a sanctuary or Holy of Holies within the Tabernacle (Exodus 25:8), Moses said in front of the Holy One Blessed be He, "Master of the Universe, the heavens and beyond cannot contain You, and You say 'Make for Me a *Mikdash*!'" The Holy One Blessed be He said to him, "Moses, it is not as you think I think. Rather lay twenty boards to the north, and twenty boards to the south, and eight to the west, and I will descend and *mitzamtzem* (contract). My *Shekhina* the Divine presence will be among you below" (Pesikta D'rav Kahana Parsha 2:10, also see Shmot Rabbah 34:1).

While our idea of work—*melacha*—is to effect change in existing material, this is the perspective of a finite human being utilizing creativity within a finite scheme of time, space, and matter. God is infinite and transcends these limitations. For God to allow His presence to dwell in this sanctuary, some type of contraction is necessary on God's part. The Kabbalists believe that creation is *yesh me'ayin*—something from nothing. They believe that there was at first *Ein Sof*, the infinite, and then God contracted, *tzimtzum*. Creation is not the result of God adding something finite; rather, it is the result of God holding back infinity, as it were.

We now see creation, and *Shabbat*, from a different perspective. On the first day, God holds back infinity; likewise on the second through sixth days. Finally, at the end of the sixth day, the world is complete and God rests. In other words, God reverts back to a non-contraction mode, back to infinity. *Shabbat* is therefore the day that represents infinity, the one day that relates to and reflects God on His terms, not via the *tzimtzum*.

While God held back in order to create, man must do the opposite: In order to create something he must go forward. While God went into His infinite mode on *Shabbat*, transcending the *tzimtzum* He employed in creating the world, man must again do the opposite. Man must hold back his creative energies. Man is said to be made in the image of God; we are, in fact, the mirror image of God, reversed so to speak. We are opposites. Therefore on *Shabbat* we "hold back" while trying to be like God in the only way which we can—by imitating God's *tzimtzum*. Our rest on *Shabbat* is a commemoration of the act of creation. We do on *Shabbat* what God did in creation.

There is an intrinsic relationship between the laws of *Shabbat* and the building of the *Mikdash*. Both represent the idea of God holding back. God practices self-control by limiting the infinite in the process of creation. *Shabbat* is a one-day adventure in choosing self-control involving even the most mundane, arguably trivial activities, only because they are defined as creative activity, *melacha*.

Both *Shabbat* and the *Mikdash* are about God dwelling in this world. By virtue of our incorporating Godliness into our lives we redeem the world —and establish a channel to the Infinite God. This is another way that God wants to be born in man's consciousness—in a house of stone, on the earth. "That you live for God," writes Jung, to Walter Robert Corti, "is perhaps the healthiest thing about you."

God wants to be born in the flame of man's consciousness, leaping ever higher. And what if this has no roots in the earth? What if it is not a house of stone where the fire of God can dwell, but a wretched straw hut that flares up and vanishes? Could God then be born? One must be able to suffer God. That is the supreme task for the carrier of ideas. He must be the advocate of the earth. God will take care of himself. My inner principle is: *Dues et homo.* God needs man in order to become conscious, just as he needs limitation in time and space. Let us therefore be for him limitation in time and space, an earthly tabernacle (Jung, *Letters,* Vol. I, 65-66).

By emulating God, exercising self control, and choosing to observe *Shabbat,* and refrain from work, a person becomes an earthly tabernacle for God. The woman who dreamt of her problem of the mouse understood that she did not want to follow the simple little mouse of instinctual sexuality into an emotional hole. Nor did she wish to remain depressed and lost in the house of *dolchi,* or sweetness, where she felt no control or understanding, or sense of personal choice. The *Torah* portion showed her another way. She, personally, could choose self control, and make a deep voluntary commitment to give the seventh day, *Shabbat,* to knowing, being, GOD.

Dreamwork and Meditation

O nce again we must return to the beginning when the *ruach* or spirit of
God moved over the astonishingly empty chaos and unformed void
(Genesis 1:2), and to the time when God blew the *chayyim Elohim*, the spirit
of life, into man (Genesis 2:7). Each time the spirit of God is breath. Every
form of meditation begins with breathing. In fact breathing is in itself the
most complete and natural form for meditation. Breathing in, deeply, allowing the breath to go down into the *hara* or place below the belly button,
and allowing the natural wave of exhalation to follow and initiate the next
inhalation. . . . this is what works best. Within moments one is at peace and
deeply connected to one's self and God. Like the simple instruction in *Zen
Mind, Beginner's Mind*, if your thoughts wander, bring them back to breathing.
One can meditate on a Hebrew letter, or sometimes on a name for God, or a
dream image. One can simply focus on a candle flame, and breathe.

One can follow a period of meditation with a particular form of dreamwork, that Jung called active imagination. This is the sort of dreamwork the
woman who dreamt of the mouse and the saffron colored cloth was doing.
It is a way of dreaming the dream onward and asking the various elements
in the dream to interact, and reveal and elucidate their meaning. The phrase
from the Book of Job:

> In a dream, in a vision of the night, when deep sleep falls upon men,
> in slumber upon the bed, He opens the ears of men, and seals their
> instruction (Job 33:15-16).

By doing truly soulful dreamwork one draws closer to God. You learn
what is the Divine instruction given in the dream. This method always yields

new meaning, and added value. It is not the reductive "wish fulfillment" method of dream interpretation used in the old Freudian approach. By drawing in the *ruach*, the spirit of God, and opening yourself to the dream's meaning you connect to your little animal soul, your *nefesh chayyim* and feel refreshed and whole.

"KNOW GOD"

This is the first commandment: to know God, and to love God. Or actually, it is the second commandment; God's first instruction is "Be fruitful and multiply"—life. The two ideas are connected by love in all it's sacred and profane ways. The Song of Songs is all about love, and mentions God not at all. Traditionally, this love song is sung on the first night of Passover: *I am the Lord your God who brought you out of slavery in the land of Egypt.* The Seder feast celebrates God who loved his people so much that he freed them from *aretz Mitzriyim*, the low narrow enslaved state in the land of Egypt. The limiting narrow confines of fear, greed, power seeking, and hate are not possible when a person is full of loving God . . . with all his heart, and with all his soul, and with all his might.

There is another key in the word, "Know God." It means know intimately and honestly and directly, GOD. It is a command to encounter, encourage, enable, entreat, and enter GOD completely. Time and place are one in this commandment. The word for giving a command and keeping the command are the same: *Mitzvah.* God commands us to keep the commandments as an act of love, not fear. Experience is required. Knowing, not faith—know God, and love God directly and personally.

Soulful dreamwork done with a heart full of courage, energy and love gives balance, harmony, melody, and rhythm.

Ahavta—"you must love"—the Hebrew word itself is an instruction manual for a breathing meditation: *Ahavta* begins with the letter *aleph*—awe א Arms raised, inhale deeply, and breathe. Next, the letter *heh*, ה—an opening. Enter. Followed by *vet* ב—an exhale, a safe house, Shelter with an open door. Freedom. Breathe in, and breathe out. Be one, whole, with God. Remember that in the beginning of creation God breathed *ruach*—spirit—over the *tohu v'bohu*—chaos and void. And then God breathed life into dust, to make *Adamah*, red earth, human. You cannot be fully human, present, authentic, and real unless you breathe properly.

Dreams are very helpful in working with one's Self. The other people in the dreams are shadow aspects of one's self. They think and behave in ways that the dreamer has not accepted or integrated into himself. Sometimes they are "good" shadows—as yet unlived aspects of one's self, and sometimes they are "bad" aspects, or black fire. Either way, one can use a process of active imagination to begin to know and love these Others. This is a truly erotic and profound way to know one's self. It is wise to begin by being asking all the people and aspects of the dream if they are willing to communicate. If they are not, the process cannot continue. One must wait until the time is right. The Bride in the Song of Songs cries:

> I adjure you, O you daughters of Jerusalem, by the gazelles, and by the hinds of the field, that you awaken not, nor stir up love, until it please (Song of Songs 3:5).

When the time is right, the real work begins. I knew a two year old little girl who traveled throughout Europe one summer with her parents. For many weeks she played in the back seat of their car with her imaginary friends, Subee and Angronck. Whenever the couple and the little girl sat down at a café table the little girl would say to her father, "Don't sit there— Angronck is sitting there!" Subee, it seemed, was always away taking a nap. One day toward the end of their journey the child became very agitated in the back seat of the car and began crying and shouting at Angronck. She told her parents: "Angronck tried to take my jewels. I had to fight with him." Jung writes in *Analytic Psychology, Theory and Practice* that in the depths of the unconscious is a treasure guarded by a serpent or a dragon. Sometimes these depths carry the image of a four gated city, or as it did for this child, a four seated café table. Jung writes:

> So these depths, that layer of utter unconsciousness in our dream, contain at the same time the key to individual completeness and wholeness...The descent into the depths will bring healing. ... This

is the place of primordial unconsciousness and at the same time the place of healing and redemption, because it contains the jewel of wholeness. It is the cave where the dragon of chaos lives and it is also the indestructible city, the magic circle . . . the sacred precinct where all the split-off parts of the personality are united. (*Analytic Psychology, Theory and Practice*, 137-138)

The sacred precinct where the personality is united. Just as I write that last line at three o'clock in the morning, a tiny ding of my computer announced an e-mail. It was a day or so before Passover and a friend wrote that each night this week she would come home and clean her house of *chamatz* (bread and cookies and cake crumbs) before the coming holiday. While doing that work, this *piyyut*, or poem, which is said near the end of the first Seder kept coming to her. Now it came to me:

> *Karev yom asher hu lo yom v'lo leilah.*
> *Ram hoda ci lecha ha yom af lecha ha leilah:*

> May a day come near which is not day or night.
> God on high, announce that—
> To you belongs the day and also the night.

The synchronicity of this little prayer coming with my friend's house work, and my writing about soulful dreamwork, lends a feeling of wholeness and meaning to the process. This is always the experience of synchronicity: It feels like a proof of God. There is a kind of reassuring comfort. One feels held in God's embrace and safe in the world of time and place.

About the Author

Dr. Barbara Black Koltuv is a clinical psychologist and a Jungian analyst. She is a graduate of the C. G. Jung Institute in New York. After receiving her Ph.D. degree from Columbia University, Dr. Koltuv graduated from the New York University Post Doctoral Program in Psychoanalysis where she studied dream work intensively with Erich Fromm.

Dr. Koltuv is the author of *The Book of Lilith*, *Weaving Woman*, *Solomon and Sheba: Individuation and Inner Marriage*, *Amulets, Talisman, and Magical Jewelry*, all published by Nicolas-Hays. Dr. Koltuv lives and is in private practice in New York city.

For further information visit *www.jungiananalystnyc.com*.